Heritage: a visitor's guide

EDITED BY
Éilis Brennan

THE OFFICE OF PUBLIC WORKS

Baile Átha Cliath
arna fhoilsiú ag Oifig an tSoláthair.

Le ceannach díreach ón
Oifig Dhíolta Foilseachán Rialtais, Teach Sun Alliance,
Sráid Theach Laighean, Baile Átha Cliath 2,
nó trí aon díoltóir leabhar.

Dublin.
Published by the Stationery Office.

To be·purchased through any Bookseller, or directly from the
Government Publications Sales Office, Sun Alliance House,
Molesworth Street, Dublin 2.

Printed in the Republic of Ireland by
Turner Print Group, Longford and Dublin

ISBN 0-7076-0102-9

DESIGN AND ORIGINATION: JARLATH HAYES
TYPESET BY REE-PRO LTD., DUBLIN
REPRODUCTION AND PLATEMAKING BY IRISH PLATEMAKING SERVICES LTD., DUBLIN, IRELAND

Contents

Acknowledgements

This guide has been produced by the Commissioners and staff of the Office of Public Works with the kind assistance of DR PETER HARBISON *and* RUTH HEARD, *who have provided material on National Monuments and Inland Waterways, respectively.*

All photographs, other than those acknowledged below are by Con Brogan, Senior Photographer with the Office of Public Works.

The Commissioners of Public Works are very grateful to the following for permission to reproduce photographs.

Airlifting materials for conservation work on Skellig Michael — THE OFFICE OF PUBLIC WORKS

Foreword

Since my appointment as Minister of State with responsibility for the Office of Public Works, I have become very much aware of the importance of the work being carried out by the Office in the protection and conservation of our national heritage.

This heritage is a rich and varied one. We are extremely fortunate in having so much of value and so many areas of great natural beauty still relatively unspoilt.

The purpose of this guide is twofold: firstly, to foster a sense of appreciation and pride in what is our inheritance with a firm determination to cherish and to protect it, and secondly, to outline some of the work that is being done by the Office of Public Works to conserve and to present this heritage.

Tá súil agam go mbainfidh tú an-phléisiúr as an eolaí seo agus go mbeidh seans agat cuairt a thabhairt ar chuid de na suímh iontacha oidhreachta atá luaite ann.

Brendan Daly

BRENDAN DALY, TD
Minister of State

Introduction

The Office of Public Works is one of the oldest state offices. It was established in 1831, with appointed Commissioners, to carry out a very wide variety of public works, such as the construction of public buildings, roads, bridges and harbours. These projects not only increased economic development during the nineteenth and early twentieth century but they also provided much-needed employment.

The present-day Office of Public Works has retained many of its original functions and has acquired new roles. It is responsible for the restoration and preservation of many prestigious state buildings, the acquisition and fitting out of office accommodation, the construction and maintenance of garda stations and prisons, and the arterial drainage programme. It also has responsibility for the protection and conservation of the National Heritage through its National Parks and Monuments, Waterways and Wildlife Services.

NATIONAL MONUMENTS

The Office of Public Works [OPW] is the principal State body with responsibility for protecting the nation's built heritage. The Irish Church Act of 1869 put the first National Monuments, which were ecclesiastical buildings, under their care. Given the abundance of monuments and archaeological sites in the country — about 120,000 — it would obviously be impossible for OPW to take on the maintenance and conservation of them all. So, over the years OPW has had to be selective. Those not maintained by the State can be protected from damage or destruction by registration and preservation orders under the National Monuments Acts, 1930 to 1987.

Most of the prime monuments and archaeological sites, are included in the collection of over 600 groups of National Monuments in the care of OPW, either by way of ownership or guardianship. The maintenance and conservation of these is a painstaking task, involving research and direction by archaeologists and architects, who are experts in the conservation of ancient structures, together with a skilled workforce using old crafts and, where appropriate, modern technology. This ensures that the monuments, which were created over the ages — in some cases, over 5,000 years ago — will be passed on to future generations to appreciate and to admire. As the recognised conservation authority, OPW endeavours, as personnel resources permit, to make professional advice of a general nature available to others contemplating work on privately-owned ancient buildings.

NATIONAL PARKS AND GARDENS

The responsibility of the Office of Public Works for parks and gardens of national importance dates back to 1860. In that year Phoenix Park was entrusted to the care of the Commissioners. Saint Stephen's Green followed some twenty years later.

Today the parks and gardens managed by the Office of Public Works range in size from a small Garden of Remembrance to our largest National Park of over 100 square kilometres. These parks and gardens are grouped into three categories: National Parks, National Heritage Gardens and National Historic Parks.

Irish national parks are wholly State-owned and they conform to strict international criteria for such parks. In these respects they differ from very large protected landscapes designated as national parks in some other countries, including England and Wales. Their essential purpose is to conserve natural plant and animal communities, scenic landscapes, which are both extensive and of national importance, and under conditions compatible with that objective to enable people to visit and to appreciate them.

There are at present three National Parks — at Killarney in Kerry, Glenveagh in Donegal and Connemara in Galway. Two others are in the process of being established in Wicklow and the Burren district in Clare. They will be featured in updated editions of this book.

Ireland's mild climate allows plants from very diverse origins to flourish side-by-side, and many fine gardens have been created. A few are now in State ownership as National Heritage Gardens. They are beautifully designed and landscaped, containing rich plant collections. Each plant is conserved and developed in accordance with its particular horticultural traditions.

There are three National Heritage Gardens. Two form part of national parks and they are described below along with the parks: Kerry's Muckross Gardens in Killarney National Park and Donegal's Glenveagh Gardens in Glenveagh National Park. The third one, Ilnacullin, is an island garden in Bantry Bay in Co. Cork.

The National Historic Parks are a diverse group, but they share the common purpose of conserving places which are of national importance as part of our historic heritage, and of enabling people to visit and appreciate them. There are at present seven such parks. Some are designed landscapes where the landscape itself is now of historic significance. Of these Phoenix Park and Saint Stephen's Green in Dublin are both long-established and well-known public parks. Two others, also in Dublin, are memorial gardens of more recent origin: the Garden of Remembrance and the War Memorial at Islandbridge.

Other parks include buildings and their grounds are associated with famous people in Irish history: Scoil Éanna (Saint Enda's) in the Dublin suburbs now houses the Pearse Museum, while Derrynane in Kerry was Daniel O'Connell's family home. Kilkenny Castle with its grounds reflects not a particular historic personage but a past way of life.

WILDLIFE

The Wildlife Service is responsible for the implementation of the Wildlife Act of 1976. This is an enormous task, spanning thousands of species and their habitats throughout the country. Protection of our wildlife can only be achieved in the context of a generally healthy living countryside. The wilder areas of natural habitat cannot be protected in isolation. It involves protecting all species of plants and animals, and the communities in which they live. Insects and other minute animals and plants are as important to the working of nature as large high-profile species. The major functions of the Wildlife Service are:

- Protection and management of sites which are important habitat for wild flora and fauna
- Species protection, including controls on the taking, hunting and trade with regard for the conservation requirements
- Promoting knowledge and awareness of the natural world through publicity and education programmes
- Involvement in international conservation efforts under European Community legislation; several international conventions and as part of programmes of the Council of Europe and other international organisations, within the framework of the World Conservation Strategy.

The objective of the habitat conservation programme is the conservation of representative ecosystem types which form the habitat of plant and animal communities.

At the time of writing a total of seventy-three areas have been given protected status, mostly as national nature reserves with a smaller number of refuges for fauna. Apart from legal protection, such areas require effective management on the ground, in accordance with a carefully designed management plan. In acquiring habitats, special emphasis has been placed on our peatland heritage of raised and blanket bogs.

Comprehensive measures are also in force for the conservation and protection of wild flora and fauna, including game, and for the regulation of trade and exploitation of species. Any wild species may be afforded 'protected' status by regulations made under the Wildlife Act. The main criteria for granting protection are the general status nationally of any population and the degree to which any existing threats may affect that status.

Where a species is protected under the terms of the Act, it is unlawful to hunt, capture or kill such species except in accordance with licences or permissions issued under the Wildlife Act for such purposes as lawful hunting, scientific research or educational objectives, or to prevent damage to crops, fisheries, livestock, etc. in certain circumstances.

Most wild mammals, birds and certain plants are now protected in Ireland. Wildfowl sanctuaries, or no-hunting areas, are also designated under the Act and there are sixty-eight of these areas throughout the country.

WATERWAYS

The Inland Waterways under the care of the Office of Public Works are the Shannon

Navigation, the Grand Canal, including the Barrow Navigation, and the Royal Canal. They form an extensive network across the country, linking Dublin and the east coast with Waterford Harbour in the south-east, the port of Limerick and the Atlantic in the west and the lakes of Leitrim and Roscommon in the north-west. Because of their linear nature they are described in a separate chapter in this guide, rather than in the regional sections, but their attractions can be appreciated by visitors to any of the points through which they pass.

While the Office of Public Works has been responsible for the maintenance of the Shannon Navigation since 1846, it was not until the passing of the Canals Act in 1986 that almost all the navigable waterways in the State were placed under one Government authority — a step which was long called for by various Government-appointed commissions.

The Act obliges the Office of Public Works to manage and to maintain the canals as a public amenity for navigation, fishing —

> 'or otherwise for the enjoyment and recreation of the public'.
> — *Canals Act 1986*

It represents a clear recognition of the present-day role of the waterways which were originally constructed as transport arteries for commercial use. They should not be regarded as of interest only to the boating fraternity.

As described in the text, the attractions of Ireland's waterways heritage are many and varied and well worth investigating.

USING THIS GUIDE

The National Monuments, Parks and Gardens, Nature Reserves and Refuges described in this book are grouped in regional chapters, corresponding to the country's tourism regions. The nature of the Inland Waterways do not lend themselves to regions, as has already been said, so they have been given a chapter to themselves.

The choice of National Monuments is limited to one hundred and is a very good cross section of all that is best in Ireland's ancient heritage. The selection ranges in time from Stone Age megalithic tombs to nineteenth-century industrial archaeology and the homes of twentieth-century patriots.

The reader may note that some very well-known National Monuments have been omitted, but it is for a variety of reasons. Bunratty Castle, while it is protected under the National Monuments Acts, is owned by Shannon Development Limited. Some have been omitted because there are problems with public access, while others are in need of major consolidation works prior to admittance of the public. Skellig Michael or Great Skellig, for example — described briefly in Wildlife — is very vulnerable to physical risks, which can arise from too many visitors, and access to it is difficult. At present there are no *licensed* boats plying to, and from, the mainland.

All the parks and gardens in this guide, which are open to visitors, are in the care of the Office of Public Works, and lands which have been acquired to form part of new parks will feature in updated editions.

The seventy-three nature reserves and refuges for fauna so far protected under the Wildlife Act are described briefly. Greater details are provided for the popular, larger and more accessible sites than for those which are small, remote or difficult to reach. Although most of these reserves are owned and managed by the Office of Public Works, a few belong to other organisations or individuals and merely receive the legal protection of the Wildlife Act.

VISITING SITES

Access to most national monuments is openly available. In other cases it can be gained by contacting the keyholder/caretaker, whose name and address will be displayed at the relevant site. OPW hopes that the visitor will understand the necessity for a keyholding arrangement for the protection of some monuments and will not be disappointed should the caretaker not be at home at the precise moment of calling.

Visitors should also be aware that OPW does not always own the land which it is necessary to cross, in order to reach particular monuments. Neither is there a public right of way in some cases. It can happen sometimes, but not often, that landowners will refuse or restrict access over the land. The same problem may arise at some nature reserves.

The maintenance and conservation of monuments, parks, reserves and waterways is a continuing and unremitting task. Should a visitor call to a site where work is in progress, it is as well to reflect on its purpose, which is that of conserving this great Irish heritage for the benefit of present and future generations. Disruption is kept to an absolute minimum.

Preservation of Ireland's heritage depends on public co-operation and it is an offence to damage or deface a national monument, or to remove or interfere with animals, plants, or their habitats, in a nature reserve, or park, or along the waterways. It is requested that all places visited be left as the visitor would wish to find them. It must also be emphasised that monuments are ancient structures and, together with parks, reserves and waterways, they contain inherent hazards. Caution must be exercised at all times. Provided a modicum of care is taken, visiting heritage destinations can be an absorbing, enjoyable, lifelong leisure pursuit.

The Office of Public Works provides interpretative services at a number of sites and some include guided tours, walks, exhibitions, audio-visual shows, self-guiding trails, booklets, leaflets and postcards. There are also restaurants, or tea-rooms, at some locations.

Visitor services are provided at twenty-one national monuments, at most parks and at a small number of reserves. The times when these services are available are outlined after the descriptions of the relevant sites.

The Office of Public Works, June 1990.

The Regions of Ireland

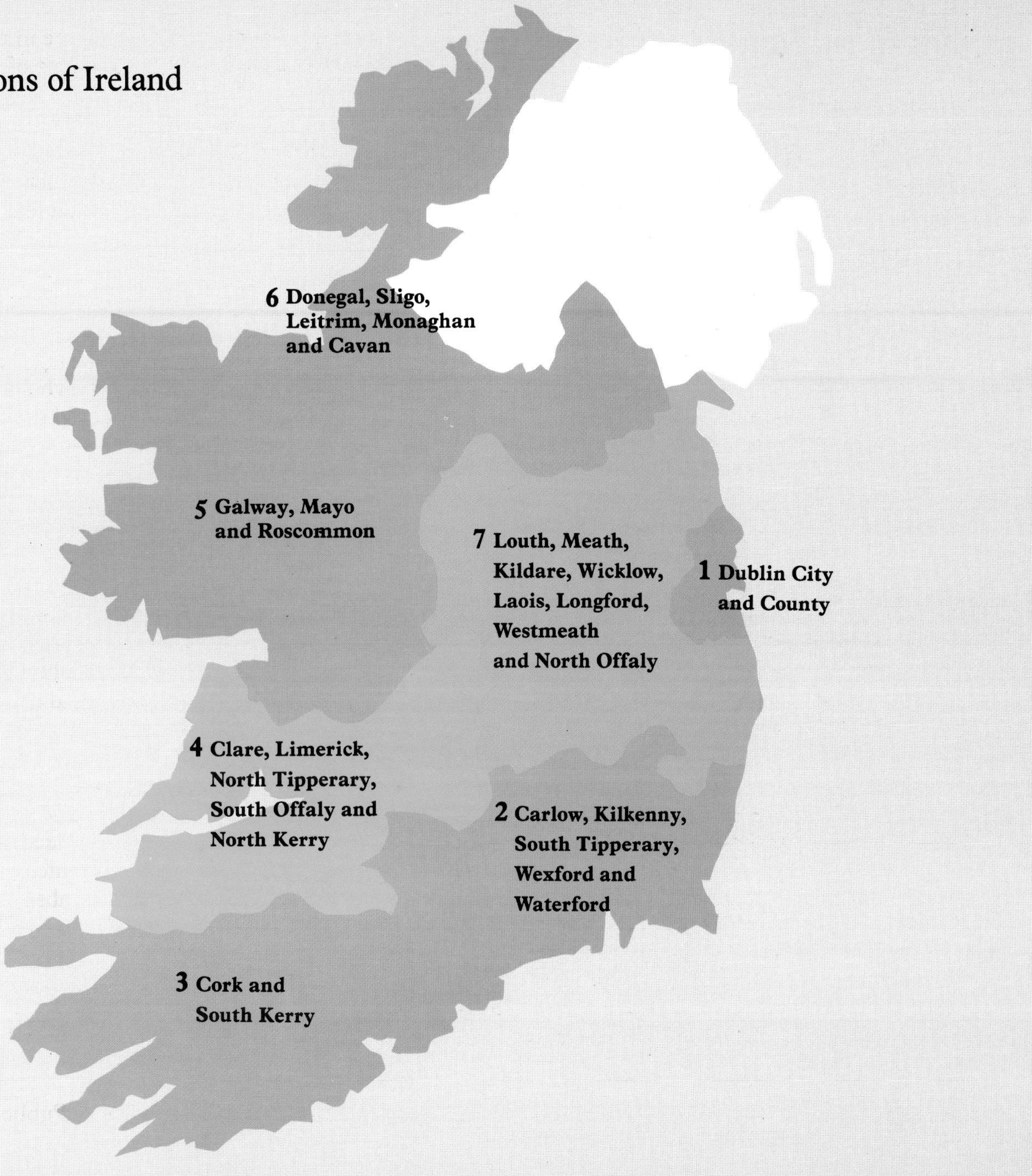

6 Donegal, Sligo,
Leitrim, Monaghan
and Cavan

5 Galway, Mayo
and Roscommon

7 Louth, Meath,
Kildare, Wicklow,
Laois, Longford,
Westmeath
and North Offaly

1 Dublin City
and County

4 Clare, Limerick,
North Tipperary,
South Offaly and
North Kerry

2 Carlow, Kilkenny,
South Tipperary,
Wexford and
Waterford

3 Cork and
South Kerry

Map Grid Reference

Sites described in this book can be located on maps using the grid reference numbers which are directly under the name of each monument, park and reserve. Four-figure grid references are generally used and enable sites to be located to the nearest kilometre.

The national grid is divided into lettered sub-zones, as shown on this diagram, each of which is a square measuring 100 kilometres in each direction. All Ordnance Survey maps and most other maps show the national grid, either as lines across the map or as numbered scales at the edge of the map from which grid references can be located.

A four-figure grid reference identifies a particular 1 km square within each sub-zone. For example, Blessington, Co. Wicklow, grid references N98 14, is 98 km east and 14 km north of the south-west (bottom left-hand) corner of sub-zone N. The first pair of figures always indicates how far east the location is, and the second pair of figures how far north it is, within the lettered sub-zone.

Two-figure grid references are used in this book for national parks and other larger areas. The principle is the same but each figure represents 10 kilometres, the first one being 10 km east and the second one being 10 km north. Taking the same example the two-figure reference for Blessington is N91.

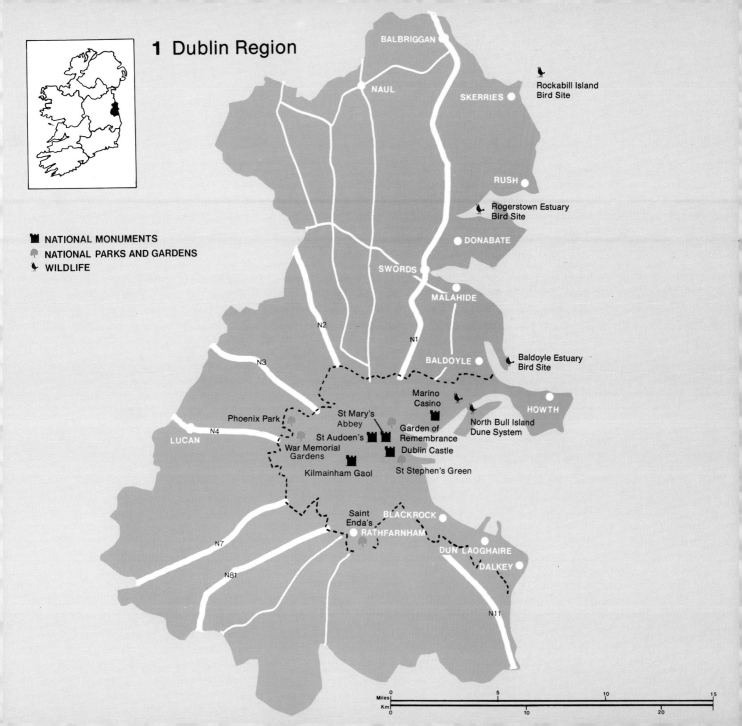

1 Dublin Region

BALBRIGGAN

NAUL

SKERRIES

Rockabill Island
Bird Site

RUSH

Rogerstown Estuary
Bird Site

DONABATE

SWORDS

MALAHIDE

N2

N3

N1

BALDOYLE

Baldoyle Estuary
Bird Site

N4

Marino
Casino

HOWTH

LUCAN

Phoenix Park

St Mary's
Abbey

Garden of
Remembrance

North Bull Island
Dune System

St Audoen's

Dublin Castle

War Memorial
Gardens

Kilmainham Gaol

St Stephen's Green

Saint
Enda's

BLACKROCK

N7

RATHFARNHAM

DUN LAOGHAIRE

N81

DALKEY

N11

■ NATIONAL MONUMENTS
🌳 NATIONAL PARKS AND GARDENS
🐦 WILDLIFE

Miles
Km

0   5   10   15

0   10   20

National Monuments

DUBLIN

Marino/Casino
O18 37

James Caulfield, 1st Earl of Charlemont (1728-1799), was one of Ireland's most 'Renaissance' men, not in period, but in his all-round accomplishments. A fine scholar and a patron of the arts, he was the first President of the Royal Irish Academy and commander-in-chief of the Irish Volunteers in the early 1780s. His Dublin town-house was what is now the Hugh Lane Municipal Gallery of Modern Art in Parnell Square, for which the architect was Sir William Chambers. What was perhaps Charlemont's greatest stroke of genius, however, was to get Chambers to design for him a small Pleasure-house, called a casino, on his estate in what was then (1758) the country, but now the suburb of Marino.

What Chambers created is one of the greatest and most refined gems of classical architecture in these islands, designed in the most up-to-date Franco-Roman neo-classical taste. Though it may seem from the outside to be merely a large one-roomed structure, it cleverly houses a total of sixteen rooms spread over three floors, of which the upper floor and basement were bedrooms and servants' quarters, respectively. The ground floor was the most important, consisting of a vestibule, central saloon and study with star-decorated ceiling. The Earl's bedroom is on the first floor.

The builder was the sculptor, Simon Vierpyl, whom Chambers had brought with him from Rome, and one of his apprentices was the famous Irish sculptor, Edward Smyth, who may have assisted in the classical sculpture of the building, including the vases on the skyline which ingeniously hide their function as chimneys.

Open daily mid-June to September. 10.00-18.00 hours.
Enquiries phone (01) 331618.

DUBLIN

Dublin Castle
O15 34

Dublin Castle was the seat and symbol of royal government in Ireland from the Norman invasion up until the establishment of the Free State in 1922. Most of the great medieval fortress has long since been replaced by a magnificent quadrangle of buildings surrounding the Upper Yard.

The medieval castle was rectangular in form with circular towers at each of the corners and was built in the early 13th century within the south-east corner of the pre-existing Viking town on foot of an order issued by King John in 1204. Of the medieval fabric only the Record Tower at the south-east corner survives but recent archaeological excavations, carried out in advance of a major rebuilding programme, uncovered remains of the other corner towers and revealed a massive moat connected to the Liffey by its tributary the Poddle. In the Viking and Norman Defences exhibition visitors can now descend beneath the rebuilt buildings and see the only remnants of the Viking town defence visible in Dublin and also features of the north-east corner of the castle including the base of the

The Casino, Marino

Kilmainham Gaol

The north side of the Upper Yard, Dublin Castle

Powder Tower and the moat with the town wall crossing it.

A disastrous fire in 1684 sealed the fate of the medieval castle and gradually the old walls were demolished and the buildings surrounding the Upper Yard built culminating about 1750 in the completion of the north side with its clock tower and matching gateways surmounted by statues. Across the yard are the State Apartments which are open to visitors. Magnificent interiors can be seen here such the Throne Room and St. Patrick's Hall which are still used for State functions as in the days prior to independence. Portions of these buildings were built and rebuilt at different times right up to the present century and the east and much of the south sides of the Upper Yard had to be rebuilt in the 1960s. A major restoration and rebuilding programme was carried out on the north and west sides of the Upper Yard in 1986-89 to accommodate a conference centre in readiness for the Irish presidency of the European Community in 1990. Not to be missed is Francis Johnston's ornate gothic revival Church of the Most Holy Trinity in the Lower Yard built around 1810 and recently restored.

Open Monday to Friday 10.00-12.15 and 14.00-17.00 hours.
Saturday, Sunday and Bank Holidays 14.00-17.00 hours.
Enquiries phone (01) 777580

DUBLIN

Kilmainham Gaol
O12 34

If for no other reason Kilmainham Gaol would be remarkable for being the biggest unoccupied gaol in either Britain or Ireland. As such, it gives the visitor a dramatic and realistic insight into what it was like to have been confined in one of these forbidding bastions of punishment and correction between 1796, when it opened, and 1924, when it closed.

The reason the gaol survives today is because of

the way in which it manages to symbolise Ireland's tradition of militant and constitutional nationalism from the rebellion of 1798 right up to the War of Independence and Civil War of 1919-23. Almost every upsurge and assertion of the Irish aspiration for political independence in that period — with the exception, perhaps, of Daniel O'Connell's Repeal Movement of the 1840s — found its echo in Kilmainham Gaol. Leaders of the rebellions of 1798, 1803, 1848, 1867 and 1916 were detained here. Robert Emmet, Anne Devlin, Thomas Francis Meagher, William Smith O'Brien, Charles Stewart Parnell, Eamon de Valera, Pearse, Connolly, Plunkett and other leaders of the 1916 Rising, all either served time or were executed within its walls.

Touching in so many crucial ways on the people and forces that shaped modern Ireland, Kilmainham Gaol offers a panoramic insight into some of the most profound, disturbing and inspirational themes of modern Irish history.

Open daily June to September 11.00-18.00 hours.
Sunday and Wednesday October to May 14.00-18.00 hours.
Booking office open all year round Monday to Friday.
Enquiries phone (01) 535984.
Literature available at site.

DUBLIN

St Audoen's Church
O15 34

Near the centre of the old Viking and medieval city of Dublin, and only a good stone's throw west of Christ Church Cathedral, is the church of St Audoen, dedicated to a saintly 7th-century bishop of Rouen whose cult may have been introduced by the men of Bristol who had been granted the city in 1172. The church was one of a group of chapels serving the Dublin craftsmen's guilds, and the nave, its oldest part, dates back to around 1200. It is now divided into two separate sections.

The first of these is the nave, roofed to serve as

The Chapter House,
St. Mary's Abbey

a place of divine worship for the Church of Ireland, and entered through a doorway of *c.* 1190-1200, beneath a tower containing the city's oldest peal of bells (1423), and the effigial tomb of Baron Portlester and his wife. The roofless second part, entered from the porch, is in the care of the Office of Public Works, and comprises St Ann and Portlester Chapels.

DUBLIN

St Mary's Abbey/Cistercian abbey
O15 35

Certain Dublin street names north of the Liffey not far from Capel Street, such as Mary Street and Abbey Street, near the fruit market, reveal the former presence in the area of what was once the largest and most important Cistercian monastery, in Ireland — St Mary's Abbey. Founded originally for the Benedictine order of Savigny in 1139, it became Cistercian eight years later, and remained such until it was dissolved by Henry VIII in 1539, in his rush to get his hands on monastic lands and treasures.

The extensive church building provided a quarry for stone used in the construction of Essex Bridge in 1676 and what may be the remains of the cloister arcade were unearthed in Cook Street, on the far side of the Liffey, in 1975. What survives of the monastery today is one small portion of the east side of the conventual buildings, a passage — known as a slype — which connected the cloister with the outside world and, more importantly, the chapter house with blocked-up lancet east windows and four bays of ribbed vaulting. This chapter house, reached from a doorway in Meeting House Lane and now housing an interpretative exhibition, experienced one of the most dramatic moments in Irish medieval history when, in the presence of the King's Council assembled there, 'Silken' Thomas Fitzgerald threw down his Lord Deputy's sword of state in an act of open defiance against Henry VIII, an event leading to an active but short-lived rebellion which ended in Thomas's own death.

Open Tuesday to Sunday mid-June to September 12.00-18.00 hours.
Enquiries phone (01) 721490.
Literature available at site.

National Parks and Gardens

*Sculpture,
Garden of
Remembrance*

DUBLIN

Garden of Remembrance
O15 35

The Garden of Remembrance, dedicated to the memory of all those who gave their lives in the cause of Irish freedom, was opened in 1966 as part of the celebrations for the Golden Jubilee of the Rising of Easter 1916. Just a few yards from the General Post Office [GPO] in O'Connell Street, headquarters of the 1916 Rising, the site was selected as the place where the Irish Volunteers were founded in 1913, and where, at the end of the Rising in Easter Week, the prisoners were held overnight in the open.

The garden was designed by Dáithí Hanly. At its centre is a sunken area around a pool, both in the shape of a cross, between lawns and trees. The floor of the pool has a mosaic pattern symbolising peace concluded. Steps lead up from the pool to a platform backed by a carved marble wall. In a pool on the platform is a large sculpture by Oisín Kelly on the theme of the Children of Lir changed into swans, inspired by the poetry of W. B. Yeats. The sunken area is lined with seats, and the garden is intended as a place of quiet remembrance and reflection.

Open during daylight hours thoughout the year.

DUBLIN

Phoenix Park, Dublin 8
O13

The historic landscape of Phoenix Park today

Fallow deer, Phoenix Park

retains many features reflecting its three centuries of existence as a park. It originated as a walled deer-park established by the Duke of Ormond about 1662, and it took its name from Phoenix House, which probably got its name from the mythical bird rather than from the Irish words *fionn uisce*, meaning 'clear water', as is often suggested. The line of the boundary wall, enclosing an area of 700 hectares, has scarcely changed since 1680. Despite many changes since then, it remains a fine example of a 17th-century deer-park.

In 1745, Phoenix Park was opened to the public by Lord Chesterfield and it has been a popular place of recreation ever since. He also made it into a landscaped parkland, creating much of the framework of the present park landscape by planting trees and laying out roads and walks. The landscape was further enhanced in the 19th-century particularly by the work of Decimus Burton. In 1860 it was the first park to come under the care of the Office of Public Works. In recent years many features of the historic landscape have been painstakingly restored, such as gas lamps, gate piers, railings and seats. Many trees have been planted to maintain and restore historic avenues and plantations.

Noteworthy buildings are located in enclosures within the park. Áras an Uachtaráin, the residence of the President, was formerly the Vice-Regal Lodge. Other historic buildings which are now in use are St Mary's Hospital, the Ordnance Survey Offices, the American Ambassador's residence, the Garda Síochána Headquarters and the Department of Defence. Ashtown Castle, the oldest historic building in the park, is being restored to its original character.

In the People's Gardens,
Phoenix Park

The People's Flower Gardens at the city end of the park, with lawns, walks, flower beds, shrubberies, a lake and a playground, constitute a more formal Victorian-style 'park within a park'. The privately-run Zoological Gardens — better known as Dublin Zoo and dating from 1831 — are also located nearby within the park, beyond the popular Band Hollow. Some of its other prominent landmarks include the tall Wellington Testimonial Obelisk, which can be seen from afar, the Phoenix Monument, the long-established kiosk tea-rooms, and the newest historic landmark — the Papal Cross — where in 1979 Pope John Paul II celebrated Mass before a million people.

The park landscape is dominated by broad expanses of grassland separated by clumps of trees

Furry Glen, Phoenix Park

Wellington Monument, Phoenix Park

containing a great variety of species. Grassland and plantations together provide excellent habitat for a herd of over 300 fallow deer, the direct descendants of the deer for which the park was created. There is a rich grassland flora, and there are a number of different ponds. The range of habitats available, particularly in the more natural western parts of the park, support a diversity of birds and mammals.

Phoenix Park has been gradually transformed through the centuries from a country estate to the west of the city, into a precious open space within a city surrounded by spreading suburbs, with its entrance only 2.5 km (1.5 miles) from Dublin's city centre. With this change, its importance as a place of recreation for Dubliners has increased. Some active sports are facilitated. There are pitches for gaelic games and soccer, and park roads are regularly used for cycling and running events. Many joggers use the park daily. Long-established minority-interest sports still feature, notably cricket and polo. But the greatest recreational use of the park by local people and visitors from far afield is for gentle exercise: walking, strolling, viewing deer, appreciating the landscape and generally relaxing.

Open all hours throughout the year.
Car access restricted at night.
Enquiries phone (01) 213021.

DUBLIN

St Stephen's Green
O16 33

St Stephen's Green today is the best-known of Dublin's city squares. In the words of the popular ballad:
> Dublin can be heaven with coffee at eleven,
> And a stroll in Stephen's Green.

The stroller in 'the Green' will find a sanctuary from the bustle of the city streets, with tree-lined walks and shrubberies, lawns bedecked with colourful flowerbeds and a waterfall filling an

Band Music,
St Stephen's Green

Bust of James
Clarence Mangan in
St. Stephen's Green

ornamental lake which is home to ducks and geese.
The bandstand features a variety of live music
throughout the summer months.

St Stephen's Green is probably Ireland's oldest
public park, laid out about 1664 as a square and
open to the public since then, except for a period
in the last century when only keyholders had
access to it. The park today is a fine example of
Victorian landscaping, as planned by Lord
Ardilaun before he had it re-opened to the public
in 1880.

St Stephen's Green echoes important events in
Irish history. It was the scene of military action
during the Easter Rising of 1916, and it contains
numerous statues and memorials to famous Irish
men and women, including Wolfe Tone, Constance
Markievicz, W. B. Yeats and James Joyce.

Open during daylight hours throughout the year.
Enquiries phone (01) 757816.
Literature available.

DUBLIN

Scoil Éanna/Saint Enda's
O14 27

Scoil Éanna now houses a museum
commemorating Patrick Pearse (1879-1916),
patriot, poet and teacher, and Willie Pearse, a
sculptor and a close associate of his brother's
throughout their short lives.

In 1910 Patrick Pearse moved his school for
boys, known in English as Saint Enda's, to this
18th-century mansion set in spacious grounds at
the foot of the Dublin mountains — then in the
country but today surrounded by spreading
suburbs. Here he put his progressive educational
ideas into practice, and it was from here that
Patrick and his brother went out to fight on Easter
Monday 1916. Both were executed for their parts
in leading the Easter Rising.

The property was bequeathed to the State by

St Stephen's Green in early autumn

Scoil Éanna/St Enda's

Mrs Margaret Pearse, as a memorial to her sons, and it passed into the care of the Office of Public Works on the death of her daughter in 1969. The house has since been fully restored. Some rooms, including Patrick Pearse's study, are presented as furnished with original objects belonging to the Pearses. An exhibition area features documents and pictures relating to Patrick Pearse and his life. The Halla Mór is once again a suitable setting for drama and musical performances.

The Wayfarer Nature Walk through the grounds and a nature centre with environmental exhibits in the courtyard behind the house continue the traditions of Patrick Pearse, whose teaching at Scoil Éanna included appreciation of nature.

The sixteen hectares of the National Historic Park include a small lake and stream, woodland walks, playing fields and a walled garden. The Pearse Museum attracts visitors from far and near but many people come just to enjoy the pleasant surroundings of the park with its facilities augmented on summer afternoons by band concerts and a tea-room in the courtyard.

Museum open daily March and April, September and October 10.00-12.00 hours and 14.00-17.30 hours.
Daily May to August 10.00-12.30 hours and 14.00-18.00 hours.
Daily February and November 10.00-12.30 hours and 14.00-16.30 hours.
Daily December to January 10.00-12.30 hours and 14.00-15.30 hours.
Park open during daylight hours.
Enquiries phone (01) 934208.
Literature available at site.

In the Pearse Museum, Scoil Éanna

Emmet's Walk, Scoil Éanna

*Aerial view of
War Memorial Gardens*

DUBLIN

War Memorial Gardens
O12 34

The War Memorial Gardens at Islandbridge, Dublin, are dedicated to the memory of the 49,400 Irish soldiers, who died in the 1914-1918 war, and they are situated on the south bank of the Liffey just across the river from the Phoenix Park.

The gardens were designed by Sir Edwin Lutyens, and construction commenced in 1931. The symmetrical, semi-circular design centres on the War Stone and two fountains on a spacious lawn. On rising ground to the south, the Great Cross stands on a flight of steps, framed by trees and shrubs. At each end of the lawn there is a pergola linking two stone bookrooms, and a sunken rose-garden. In one of the four bookrooms are illuminated volumes containing the names of the 49,400 Irishmen and, in another, is a wooden cross first erected between the battlefields of Guillemont and Ginchy where many Irishmen died. Between the formal part of the memorial and the river, gentle slopes are traversed by tree-lined roads and are planted with flowering cherries along with other trees and shrubs.

The gardens are not only a place of remembrance, but also are of architectural interest, of great beauty at all seasons and they were fully restored in 1987-89.

The Office of Public Works manages them, in consultation with the Irish National War Memorial Committee, on behalf of the Government which is responsible for maintaining them in perpetuity.

Open during daylight hours throughout the year.

Wildlife

Baldoyle Estuary
O25 41

This tidal bay is situated north-east of Dublin city. It is a reserve with a rating of international importance for brent geese.

It is easily accessible from the public roadway.

North Bull Island
O22 37

North Bull Island is situated in the northern part of Dublin Bay within the city boundary and is only 8 km from the city centre. It is covered with dune grassland. An extensive salt marsh lies to the

*Rogerstown Estuary
Co. Dublin*

Bull Island, Co. Dublin

north-west and, at extreme low tides, these are large mud flats between the island and the mainland.

This area is of international importance for brent geese and, probably, has the highest concentration of wildfowl and waders of any Irish wetland. These include sanderling, knot, curlew, dunlin, redshank, oystercatcher, shelduck, wigeon, teal, shoveler, to name but a few. These species are easily seen from the roadway especially during the winter months.

The island also contains important plant species, such as glasswort, sea lavender and sea aster. The main area covered by the nature reserve is owned and managed by Dublin Corporation. The remainder is State-owned foreshore.

There is an interpretative centre for visitors.

Rockabill, Co. Dublin

CO. DUBLIN

Rockabill Island
D32 62

Comprising the two islands of Rockabill Island, the northern one is known as 'The Bill' and the southern one as 'Light House Island'. It is situated approximately 8 km seaward from Skerries in Dublin. As a breeding site for roseate terns, it is the most important in Europe.

It may be observed from boats but access to it is only permitted for serious research purposes by prior permission.

CO. DUBLIN

Rogerstown Estuary
O23 52

This estuary is a small tidal bay in north Co. Dublin, approximately 15 km from Dublin city, and is one consisting of several small rivers/ streams which flow in at the western and north-western sides. It is a site of international importance for brent geese.

Access to the estuary is by good perimeter roads.

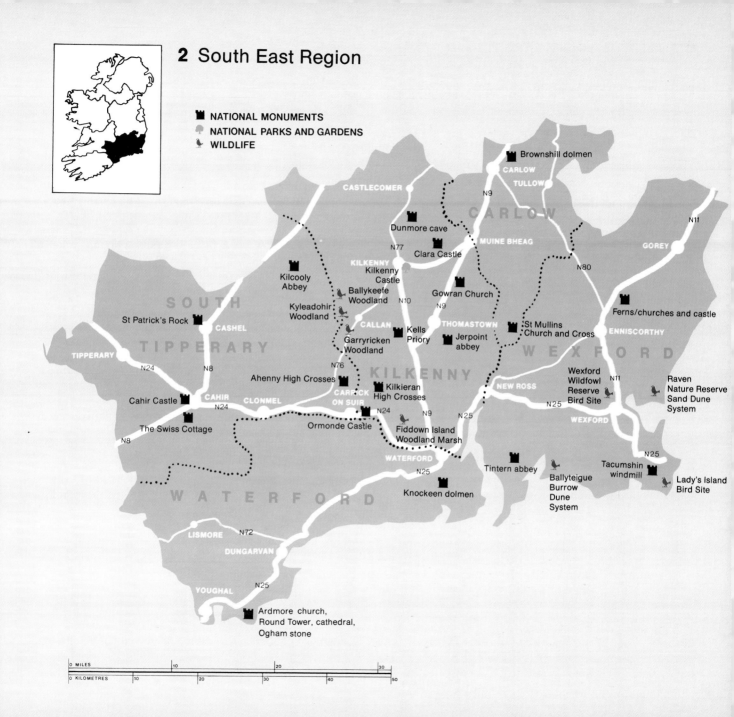

2 South East Region

- ■ NATIONAL MONUMENTS
- ♣ NATIONAL PARKS AND GARDENS
- 🐦 WILDLIFE

Brownshill dolmen

CARLOW

CARLOW

TULLOW

N9

MUINE BHEAG

N11

Dunmore cave

N77

GOREY

Clara Castle

KILKENNY

Kilkenny
Castle

Kilcooly
Abbey

N80

ENNISCORTHY

Gowran Church

Ballykeefe
Woodland

N10

Kyleadohir
Woodland

N9

Ferns/churches and castle

St Patrick's Rock

CASHEL

CALLAN

Kells
Priory

THOMASTOWN

St Mullins
Church and Cross

WEXFORD

Garryricken
Woodland

Jerpoint
abbey

TIPPERARY

SOUTH

TIPPERARY

N24

N8

Wexford
Wildfowl
Reserve
Bird Site

N11

Raven
Nature Reserve
Sand Dune
System

N76

KILKENNY

Ahenny High Crosses

CARRICK
ON SUIR

Kilkieran
High Crosses

NEW ROSS

N25

Cahir Castle

CAHIR

CLONMEL

N24

N24

N9

N25

WEXFORD

N8

The Swiss Cottage

N24

Ormonde Castle

Fiddown Island
Woodland Marsh

N9

N25

Tacumshin
windmill

N25

WATERFORD

N25

Tintern abbey

Lady's Island
Bird Site

Knockeen dolmen

Ballyteigue
Burrow
Dune
System

WATERFORD

LISMORE

N72

DUNGARVAN

YOUGHAL

N25

Ardmore church,
Round Tower, cathedral,
Ogham stone

0 MILES   10   20   30

0 KILOMETRES   10   20   30   40   50

National Monuments

CARLOW

Browneshill/Portal-tomb
S75 77

There are few more impressive witnesses to the aspirations of Stone Age man than the capstone of Browneshill portal-tomb, sited on the ridge of a hill overlooking the Barrow valley about a mile east of Carlow town. This massive stone is reputed to weigh 100 tonnes, and one can but marvel at the ingenuity of a people who attempted, 4,000 years ago, to hoist it upon the few upright stones which keep one end of it raised skywards. The other end of the capstone is still firmly stuck in the earth, either because it fell in the intervening period, or because the stone outweighed the builders' ambitions to raise it totally off the ground.

The word dolmen, derived from two Breton words, meaning stone table, was used by early antiquarians as a generic term for monuments, such as Browneshill, because they believed them to have been tables for druidical sacrifices. But we know today that they were built to provide a permanent abode for the remains of the Stone Age dead which were interred within.

CARLOW

St Mullin's/monastic site
S73 38

The last page of the 8th/9th-century *Book of Moling*, preserved in the library of Trinity College, Dublin, presents us with what has been widely taken to be the earliest-known plan of an old Irish monastery. It may even be a somewhat schematised plan of that very monastery in Co. Carlow which still bears the saint's name in a slightly modified form — St Mullin's.

The manuscript plan marked the location of sixteen crosses, but today only one small granite cross, bearing a crucifixion scene, survives on this sylvan monastic site on the spur of a small plateau overlooking the River Barrow. Nearby is a tiny oratory, known as St James's Chapel, in which we may suspect stood the tomb-shrine of the saint. Adjacent to it is the stump of a Round Tower, the medieval nave-and-chancel abbey church next to its more recent Church of Ireland counterpart, and a 16th-century building (a gaol?) known as 'The Bath'.

The modern graveyard, in which these buildings lie and where there is a remarkable collection of early 19th-century carved tombstones, is overlooked by a large grass-grown motte, a reminder that the peace of the place was once disturbed by the early Norman invaders, who placed a now-vanished wooden tower on top of the motte to establish their domination of this agriculturally-rich county.

KILKENNY

Clara Castle
S57 58

After the 13th century, when the Normans built very large-scale castles, the later medieval period saw the construction of towers of a much more modest scale, which served as the fortified dwellings of local landed families. These tower-houses survive in their many hundreds from the 15th and 16th centuries, but as their builders were more interested in defending themselves than in preserving historical records, we often know little more than the name of the family which built them. Such is the case with one of the best-preserved tower-houses in the country — Clara Castle in Co. Kilkenny.

It was presumably built by the Shortall family, and was lived in as late as 1905. From its outward-sloping base, it rises in four storeys to a height of 18.9 m. With few exceptions, the windows are all original and well-preserved, and the tower is well provided with musketry loops which suggest a date scarcely before the second half of the 16th century, when the use of guns was becoming more widespread. The walled forecourt protecting the entrance is a slightly later addition.

KILKENNY

Dunmore/cave
S51 65

Caves are frequently found in the limestone areas of Ireland. An example in State-ownership is Dunmore, located in an isolated outcrop on the

The Market Cross Dunmore Cave

35

Castlecomer plateau, only seven miles north of Kilkenny. It may not be the most extensive of the country's caves — that distinction belongs to Pollnagollum in Co. Clare, which is seven miles long — but the installation of lighting and the construction of paths and catwalks to facilitate the visitor along its quarter mile of passages allows the public to experience something of the delights of potholing.

The highlight of the calcite formations inside is the so-called Market Cross, a calcite pillar 4.57 m and 1.22 m in diameter. Called in Irish *Dearc Fearna*, the cave is known in ancient legend as one the three darkest places in Ireland, and its darkest hour came in the year 928 when the Vikings slaughtered many Irish people who had taken refuge there, and whose bones were uncovered in the course of scientific excavations during the 1970s. In the fight, one of the marauders must have dropped a bag of coins which also came to light. Some were from north-eastern England, but others were of silver, which Viking trade had brought all the way from Baghdad.

Copies of the coins, and other finds from the excavations, are now displayed in the visitor centre which stands above the cave's entrance.

Open daily mid-June to mid-September. 10.00-18.30 hours.
Tuesday to Saturday mid-March to mid-June. 10.00-13.00 hours and 14.00-17.00 hours.
Sunday 14.00-17.00 hours.
Winter opening weekends, Saturday, Sunday, public holidays. 10.00-17.00 hours.
Enquiries phone (056) 67726.
Literature available at site.

KILKENNY

Gowran Church
S63 53

This fine church dedicated to the Blessed Virgin is one of a small number of 13th-century parish churches, which are usually found in Anglo-Norman towns. Gowran Church is also called the Collegiate Church, relating to a college of chaplains founded there in 1312.

It consisted of a chancel and aisled nave with a tower which was added in the 15th century.

A 19th-century church occupies the site of the chancel. The nave is richly ornamented, with decorative windows and use of carved foliage on capitals. The north aisle arcade remains, with its pillars of quatrefoil plan.

A 17th-century chapel was built against the southwest corner of the nave. The nave and tower contain some very fine carved effigies and tombstones from the 13th to the 17th centuries, as well as an early cross inscribed Ogham Stone. Gowran Church was the burial place of the Earls of Carrick and Ormond, and other local notable families.

KILKENNY

Jerpoint/Cistercian abbey
S57 40

South of Thomastown in Co. Kilkenny is a tall, square tower which belongs to the Cistercian abbey of Jerpoint. It was originally a Benedictine monastery founded by Donal Mac Gillapatrick, King of Ossory in 1158, and came into the possession of the Cistercians in 1180.

Though the church is now fragmentary, it still preserves the stout Romanesque pillars of the original 12th-century structure, and the fine chancel, where some medieval painted armorial bearings have recently been brought to light and restored. Within the church there are also many interesting burial monuments dating from the 13th to the 16th centuries.

The abbey is unique in having the most decorative cloister arcade of any Irish church, bearing a number of secular and religious carved figures, which show us details of the clothing and armour worn in Ireland during the 15th and 16th centuries. The Cistercians may have departed four

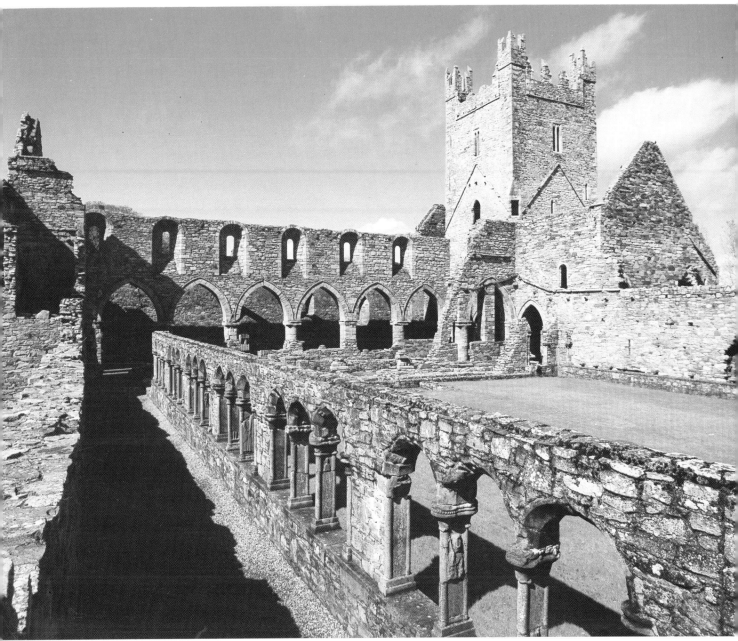

Jerpoint Abbey

and a half centuries ago, but the church and cloister, which are no longer in religious use, still breathe the peaceful and prayerful atmosphere of its former incumbents.

Beside the car park is the recently-built visitor centre.

Open daily mid-June to mid-September 10.00-18.00 hours.
Tuesday to Saturday May to mid-June 10.00-13.00 hours and 14.00-17.00 hours.
Sunday 14.00-17.00 hours.
Enquiries phone (056) 24623.
Literature available at site.

Kells Priory

KILKENNY

Kells/Augustinian priory
S50 43

Kells in Co. Kilkenny presents the visitor with an even greater surprise than does its more famous namesake in Co. Meath. On approaching from the road, one could be forgiven for thinking that ahead lay a large medieval castle, with tall and ominous walls interspersed at intervals with defensive towers. But these powerful defences, covering five acres, protect not a castle but a fortified Augustinian priory, which forms the most extensive monastic enclosure in Ireland.

The priory was founded by Geoffrey Fitzrobert in 1183 but, though the buildings are difficult to date, they are most likely to have been constructed some centuries later. The church was originally cruciform, or cross-shaped, in plan, with a Lady Chapel to the north-east. Attached to the church are two towers, both of which were presumably for domestic purposes. Sadly, the church has not withstood the test of time as well as the much-better preserved courtyard walls.

KILKENNY

Kilkieran/High Crosses
S42 27

Kilkieran, which dominates the Suir valley north of Carrick-on-Suir from its hill-side slopes, is noted particularly for its collection of High Crosses, and it is all the more remarkable, therefore, that no history of the place has been handed down to us — not even to the extent of telling us about the Kieran from whom it gets its name.

Not even a portion of a church survives, though it probably once stood on the site now occupied by a comparatively modern family burial-place roughly at the centre of the churchyard. Close to it is the West Cross, which is similar to those at Ahenny not far away in having its surface decorated with closely-meshed interlace ornament, panels of spiral and animal ornament, and large rounded bosses, all enclosed in strongly-protruding frames. The only figure sculpture comprises the horsemen on the east face of the base, the other faces bearing interlace which goes wrong in places, showing that even High Cross carvers were only human. The strange cap is difficult to explain.

Further east is a similar undecorated cross, and another High Cross unique in Ireland in having lightly-incised ornament and short, stumpy arms looking as if they were imitated from some metal prototype or other.

TIPPERARY

Ahenny/High Crosses
S41 29

For an Early Christian site which has no recorded history, it is surprising that Ahenny, otherwise known as Kilclispeen, preserves two of the most remarkable of Ireland's High Crosses.

Both of the crosses, erected in the 8th or 9th century, bear beautifully executed interlace, spiral and other geometrical ornament which spreads over the surfaces like a gossamer web, the North Cross having, in addition on its west face, a slightly awkward human interlace. This varied ornament, together with the five prominent bosses on each face, strongly suggest that both crosses were imitated from metalwork crosses which may once have existed on the site. Very different in character are the bases of the crosses, bearing figure sculpture which is clearest on the North Cross. On it we can see *The Raised Christ* on the west face with what is thought to be *The Lord creating the birds and the beasts* or *Adam naming the animals* back to back with, on the east face, a chariot procession perhaps representing *David bringing the body of Goliath to Jerusalem* on the south side, and a chariot procession on the north side.

The sculpture on the base of the south cross is sadly much more weather-worn, but *Daniel in the Lions' Den* is likely to occupy one of the panels on the east side.

High Cross, Kilkieran

TIPPERARY

Cahir/Castle
S05 25

Cahir Castle is not only one of the largest and best preserved castle in the country, but it is also one of the most easily accessible because of its position beside the road from Dublin to Cork. This was, of course, not always the case, as fortifications by their very nature were designed to keep undesirable visitors out!

The first castle on this naturally-protected island in the River Suir dates from the 13th century, but most of what survives today dates to the 15th and 16th centuries, built by the Cahir branch of the Butlers, one of medieval Ireland's great Anglo-Norman families. The stout curtain wall, with square or rounded bastions at the

Cahir Castle

corners, acted as the outer defences for the tall keep, which has been splendidly restored. Nearby is a fine hall, largely rebuilt in the 1840s. Both the keep and hall are furnished with period furniture.

But stout as the defences may have been, they proved no match for the cannon and culverin of the English Queen Elizabeth I's favourite, the Earl of Essex, in 1599, and some cannon balls still remain embedded in the castle walls as a grim reminder of his successful siege. Cromwell had it easier 50 years later, for he was able to take the castle without a single shot being fired.

The National Monuments of the region are introduced to the visitor by way of an audio-visual presentation in Cahir Cottage, which is at the far end of the outer ward of the castle defences.

Open daily May to mid-June and mid-September-end September 10.00-18.00 hours.
Tuesday to Saturday October to April 10.00-13.00 hours and 14.00-16.00 hours.
Sunday 14.00-17.00 hours.
Tuesday to Saturday November to April 10.00-13.00 hours and 14.00-16.30 hours.
Sunday 14.00-16.30 hours.
Enquiries phone (052) 41011.
Literature available at site.

TIPPERARY

Cahir/The Swiss Cottage
S05 28

A 19th-century *cottage orné* has long been known as the Swiss Cottage because of its resemblance to an alpine chalet. The first *cottage orné* was devised and built by the hapless French Queen, Marie-Antoinette, so that she could play at the game of rural cottages in the field in front of her Parisian palace. The idea quickly caught on in England and Ireland, and the Cahir example is generally recognised as one of the most perfect of its kind in these islands.

It was built *c.* 1810 for the dashing young Richard Butler, Lord Cahir, by the famous architect John Nash, who went on to build a more extravagant example for the Prince Regent in Windsor Park only a few years later.

The cottage is superbly sited with sylvan backdrop on a terrace above the River Suir, only a little more than a mile south of the town. It is a long building decorated with stick-work trellises on its verandahs and, from under an incredibly thick and beautifully-restored roof of thatch, the first-floor windows appear like eyes peering from beneath bushy eye-brows. Inside, a remarkable job of preservation and restoration in exquisite taste has been done — the dining room, with its Parisian wallpaper of 1816 showing Turks smoking on the banks of the Bosphorus, being particularly noteworthy.

Swiss Cottage, Cahir

*Ormond Castle,
Carrick-on-Suir*

Open Tuesday to Sunday mid-June to September 10.00-18.00 hours. No bus tours on Sunday.
Enquiries phone (052) 41144.
It can be seen by appointment during the off season.

TIPPERARY

Carrick-on-Suir/Ormond Castle
S40 22

This Elizabethan-style manor house was built onto an earlier castle at the eastern end of the town beside the River Suir. The house has two storeys and an attic floor with many gables and windows. It was built by Thomas Butler, 10th Earl of Ormond from 1565 onwards. Portraits of both the Earl and Queen Elizabeth I of England may be seen in the entrance passage.

The most remarkable feature of the house is its plasterwork, stucco decoration and a ground floor room decorated with coats of arms of the Ormond family. The Long Gallery on the first floor, which is approximately 30 m long, has the best

St Patrick's Rock, Cash

plasterwork and the friezes and ceilings have been fully restored and the room has been furnished. The frieze on the upper part of the walls is decorated with alternating medallion panels of King Edward VI, Elizabeth I and the royal coat of arms. All are flanked with pilasters and stucco figures of Equity and Justice. In this room there is also a very fine stone fireplace dated 1565.

Inserted in the tower of the older castle there is a blocked window with carved angels. Cromwell's troops took and occupied the castle in 1649.

Open daily mid-June to mid-September 10.00-18.00 hours.
Enquiries phone (051) 40787.
Literature available at site.

TIPPERARY

Cashel/St Patrick's Rock
S07 41

Standing on a rock, which rises dramatically from the Golden Vale, is the most imposing cluster of medieval monuments in the country. As the name Cashel [Lat. *castellum*] suggests, it was originally a strong fortification, and seat of the kings of south Munster until handed over to the church in 1101.

With the possible exception of the Round Tower, the oldest surviving building is also one of its most notable — the sandstone Cormac's Chapel, named after Cormac Mac Carthaig, King of Munster, and probably the first Irish church to have been built in the Romanesque style. It has many unique features, including two square towers in place of transepts, multi-storeyed blind arcading of the south wall, as well as a stone roof with a croft beneath, and in the chancel it preserves the only Romanesque frescoes known to have survived in this country. Unusually for an Irish church, Cormac's Chapel has no west doorway; instead, it has one minor entrance in the south wall, and two major doors on the north side, suggesting that the chapel looked northwards to some feature or structure later replaced by the large limestone

cathedral built by successive Irish archbishops in the 13th century.

The cathedral, which has interesting carved faces on the corbels, has at the west end of the nave a castle designed to protect an archbishop in the 14th century. The cathedral was set on fire in the late 15th century by the Earl of Kildare who thought that the archbishop was inside!

In front of the entrance to the castle/cathedral is a replica of the 12th-century St Patrick's Cross, the original of which was moved recently to the newly-restored and furnished 15th-century Hall of the Vicars' Choral, through which access is now gained to the Rock.

Open daily mid-March to early June 9.30-17.30 hours.
Daily June to mid-September 9.00-19.30 hours.
Daily mid-September to mid-March 9.30-16.30.
Enquiries phone (062) 61437.
Literature available at site.

TIPPERARY

Kilcooly Abbey/Cistercian abbey
S29 58

The Cistercian abbey of Kilcooly — *de Arvi Campo* — was founded in 1184 by Donal Mór O'Brien, King of Thomond. The abbey was a daughter house of Jerpoint Abbey, Co. Kilkenny (see p. 36 above). Originally built around 1200, in 1445 it was burned and almost destroyed.

In the subsequent reconstruction, a north transept and tower were added to the original Cistercian plan. The fine stone details date from this time, including the two stone sedilia for abbot and prior, and the traceried windows. A most unusual feature is the polished limestone carved panel of the wall between the transept and the sacristy, depicting the crucifixion, St Christopher and a mermaid with a mirror, as well as coats of arms. The chancel contains interesting tombs, including the 16th-century effigy of Piers Fitz Oge Butler by the sculptor Rory O'Tunney.

Near the church stands a domed columbarium or dove-cote.

WEXFORD

Ferns/churches and castle
T01 50

For a small town of its size, Ferns has a remarkable number of historical monuments which are spread over a considerable area. It was in these rich agricultural lands of north Wexford that St Aedan, or M'Aedhoc, chose to found a monastery *c.* 600, which later became the burial place of the kings of Leinster who helped to found it. The site is now marked by the Church of Ireland Cathedral, which is an early 19th-century building incorporating parts belonging to the 13th century. Seventy-five yards to the east is a further 13th-century structure looking like a chancel, but how it related to the original Norman cathedral is uncertain.

The churchyards surrounding the cathedral contain fragments of a number of decorated, or undecorated, granite High Crosses of uncertain date. In the adjoining field to the south is a church with a tower at the western end, a replacement of an abbey burned down only two years after its foundation by the ill-starred Dermot MacMurrough Kavanagh, who has gone down in history as the villain who introduced the Normans into Ireland.

It was one or other of those Normans who chose a site near the southern end of the town to build a strong 13th-century castle surrounded by a rock-cut ditch, and which has interesting remnants of a chapel on the first floor.

WEXFORD

Tacumshin/windmill
T08 07

The Office of Public Works' first venture into the realm of industrial archaeology was the taking into guardianship of Tacumshin windmill. The flat land around Tacumshin in south Wexford provides little

Tacumshin Windmill

Tintern Abbey

falling water to turn a mill-wheel, but plenty of sea-breezes to keep a windmill whirring. So, in 1846, the millwright Nicholas Moran was commissioned to build this windmill, though it may have taken almost a decade to complete.

Tacumshin is a three-storey tower mill of 17th-century design, originating in the days before the industrial revolution, though it was partially modernised when parts of a disused mill of a more up-to-date type from Ballyfane were inserted in the 1930s. The mill was operational until 1936, and was the last complete windmill in Ireland forty years ago. Partially reconstructed in 1952, one of its attractive features is the thatched roof, matched in this respect by only one other windmill in these islands, at Ballycopeland in Co. Down.

Tintern/Cistercian abbey
S79 10

The Cistercian abbey of Tintern, the centrepiece of a fine wooded estate at the top of Bannow Bay between Wellington Bridge and Duncannon, derives its name from Tintern Major in Monmouthshire, Wales, from whence monks came to people the monastery founded in 1200 by William Marshall, Earl of Pembroke. He was thereby fulfilling a promise he had made to himself during a violent storm that he would found a monastery if he survived the shipwreck which threatened him in crossing the Irish Sea.

The large church appears not to have been built until about a century after William's initial foundation. After the Dissolution of the Monasteries *c.* 1540, the abbey's lands and buildings passed to the Colclough family who, in various stages, adapted parts of the church and tower for their own domestic use, and lived there until 1963.

The most recent domestic alterations have been removed and archaeological excavations were carried out prior to the conservation works.

Ardmore/church, Round Tower, cathedral, Ogham stone
X19 77

The smallest building at Ardmore is pointed out as the tomb-shrine of the saint whose name is closely associated with the site — St Declan. He is reputed to have been one of the four missionaries who worked to christianise Ireland before St Patrick, and Ardmore's position close to the 'Celtic Sea', overlooking the fine beach of Ardmore Bay, would suggest that his connections may have been with south-western Britain.

From a distance, the most obvious monument is the tall and graceful 12th-century four-storeyed Round Tower rising to a height of 28.96 m, probably one of the last — and certainly one of the finest — to be built.

Though not a bishopric for very long, Ardmore has an interesting cathedral, constructed in various stages over a period of five centuries, though the major parts date from either side of 1200. Its most intriguing feaure is the 12th-century sculpture, possibly removed from another church and inserted into arcades on the exterior west wall. One clearly recognisable scene is the *Adoration of the Magi.*

The nave houses one of those rare Ogham stones which have the inscription going up one side and down the other.

Knockeen/Portal-tomb
S57 07

Knockeen is the most impressive portal-tomb in the county, with tall uprights supporting two capstones, one partially overlapping with the other. It is not without justification that the achievement of Stone Age people in raising such monuments to house their dead, with little technical aid other than sheer muscle, has been compared to the sending of a rocket to the moon in our own time. The likelihood is that this feat was carried out by raising up the massive covering stones, each weighing many tonnes, along the ramp of an earthen mound, which was presumably removed once the capstones had successfully been laid in place.

Such portal-tombs form a dignified and attractive contrast to the larger-scale passage and court-tombs which may have marginally preceded the period of their construction, probably around the third millennium BC.

National Parks and Gardens

KILKENNY

Kilkenny Castle
S51 56

For eight hundred years Kilkenny Castle has dominated Kilkenny City from a rocky height beside the River Nore. A four sided stone castle with towers at each corner was probably built in the early 13th century. Two centuries later it was acquired by one of the Butlers, Earls and, later, Dukes of Ormond.

Kilkenny Castle from the Rose Garden

As the Butler home for 550 years it experienced two periods of great prosperity. The first was as the elegant chateau of James, Duke of Ormond in the Restoration period of the late 17th century. The second was as a great country house in the 19th century when the castle was rebuilt to its present form, comprising the east wing with its great picture gallery and two other wings linking the three surviving corner towers of the Norman castle. It remained the home of the Butlers until 1935 and came into State care in 1969.

The east wing mainly comprises the Long Gallery, built in the 19th century and now fully restored and housing the Butler family collection of portraits and tapestries. Other rooms in this wing are open to visitors also, including the modern Butler Art Gallery and the castle kitchen, now a restaurant in summer. Structural repairs to the remainder of the castle are under way, and they will make the restoration of the great drawing room and some bedrooms possible, along with provision of new facilities for visitors.

The castle, together with its twenty-three hectares of grounds, is now a National Historic Park. The park landscape includes fine mature trees, woodland walks, an artificial lake, and magnificent sweeping tree-lined vistas to, and from, the castle, as well as a formal terraced garden at the other side of it.

Open daily April to May 10.00-17.00 hours.
Daily June to September 10.00-19.00 hours.
Tuesday to Saturday November to March 10.30-12.45 hours. and 14.00-17.00 hours.
Sunday 11.00-12.45 hours and 14.00-17.00 hours.
Enquiries phone (056) 21450.
Literature available at site.

Long Gallery, Kilkenny Castle

Wildlife

KILKENNY

Ballykeefe
S41 51

This nature reserve is 6 km north of Callan and it is a good example of young quasi-natural elm/ash/oak woods on fertile soil.

KILKENNY

Fiddown Island
S47 20

This is a long narrow island of marsh-woodland on the River Suir. It is covered in willow scrub and bordered by reed swamps — the only known

Ballyteige Burrow
Co. Wexford

site of its type in Ireland.

There is no public access, but the island is easily viewed from the public roadway.

KILKENNY

Garryricken
S40 38

Situated 5 km north-west of Callan, this reserve, like Ballykeefe above, is another good example of quasi-natural woods.

KILKENNY

Kyleadohir
S37 42

This reserve is situated 5 km south-west of Callan and is of the very same kind as Ballykeefe and Garryricken.

All three reserves, Ballykeefe, Garryricken and Kyleadohir, constitute some of the largest woods of their kind left in Ireland.

WEXFORD

The Raven Nature Reserve
T11 23

Situated 8 km north-east of Wexford town, access to it is via Wexford Wildfowl Reserve. It is a large well-developed sand dune ecosystem and consists of a forestry plantation, foreshore and seabed. The dune system has a well-developed dune vegetation, including rare plant species, such as lesser centuary [*Centuarium pilchellum*], wild asparagus [*Asparagus officinalis* ssp *prostratus*], round-leaved wintergreen [*Pyrola rotundifolia* ssp *maritima*] and yellow birdnest [*Monotropa hypopitys*].

The invertebrate fauna is also of considerable interest. The sandbanks at the southern tip provide roosting for large flocks of Greenland white-fronted geese and wading birds. Several species of tern breed on the beach at the southern end.

This reserve is open at the same hours as that of

Wexford Wildlife Reserve, Co. Wexford

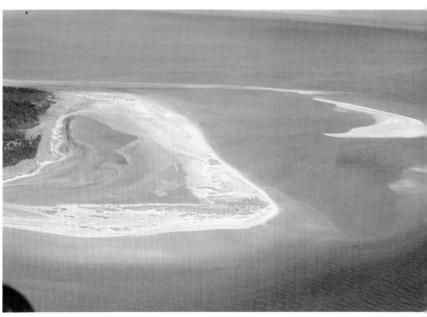

Raven Wood, Co. Wexford

Cottonweed at Lady's Island Lake, Co. Wexford

Wexford Wildfowl Reserve and there is a good internal road system with car-parking facilities.

WEXFORD

Wexford Wildfowl Reserve
T08 34

This reserve is situated on the sloblands north of Wexford Harbour. The entrance to it is by Ardcavan Lane, 1.2 km north of Wexford town on the Wexford/Castlebridge/Gorey road (L29).

The reserve, which is owned jointly with the Irish Wildbird Conservancy, forms a wintering ground of international importance for several migratory waterfowl species, in particular the Greenland white-fronted goose and greylag, pink-footed and Canada geese. Many duck species and waders occur on the reserve and can be observed in the summer and winter months.

Visitor services include a good access road, car-parking facilities and a picnic area; a wildfowl collection, bird hides and an observation tower. There is a small reception centre with interpretative material, and it is open daily from 9.00 to sunset, except for some Saturday mornings between October and January.

WEXFORD

Ballyteige Burrow
S93 06

This burrow is a 9 kilometre-long shingle spit

running north-west from the coastal village of Kilmore Quay in south Co. Wexford and adjoining foreshore.

The flora of Ballyteige Burrow includes a number of rare plants, such as wild asparagus [*Asparagus officinalis*], and it is especially rich in dune plants and those which prosper in coastal habitats.

It is accessible at all times, but there are no visitor services. Large groups are not encouraged due to the fragile nature of the dune systems.

WEXFORD

Lady's Island Lake
T10 06

Situated approximately 15 km south of Wexford town and eastwards from Kilmore Quay, this refuge for fauna is centred on two islands in Lady's Island Lake — namely Inish and Sgarbheen.

While the lake itself is an attractive habitat for a variety of waterfowl, these two islands are particularly important as a breeding ground for terns. Together they hold the largest breeding colonies of these birds in the Republic of Ireland and are the only sites known at which all five species are found breeding together. They are common species, like arctic, sandwich, roseate and little tern and there is an on-going management programme for these terns at the sites.

The islands and terns may be viewed from the pathway around Lady's Island Lake but access to the islands themselves is very restricted during the late spring/summer period to prevent disturbance.

Five species of gulls also nest here, namely great black-backed, lesser black-backed, black-headed, common and herring, and it is the only site where gadwall breed regularly in this country.

These birds can be observed from public roads but access is only permitted for serious research purposes and with prior permission.

Greenland white-fronted geese

Pine marten

Fox

Badger

Brown hare

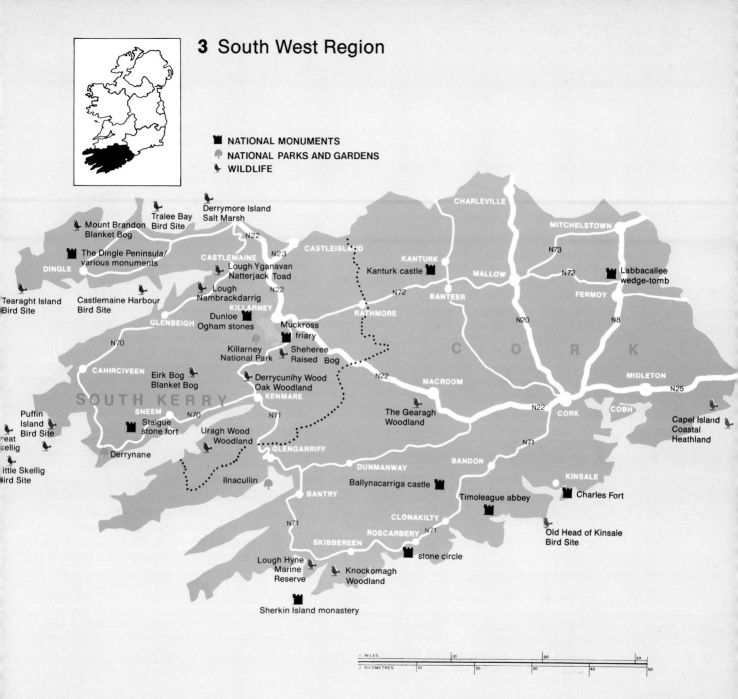

3 South West Region

NATIONAL MONUMENTS
NATIONAL PARKS AND GARDENS
WILDLIFE

Mount Brandon Blanket Bog

Tralee Bay Bird Site

Derrymore Island Salt Marsh

The Dingle Peninsula/ various monuments

DINGLE

Castlemaine Harbour Bird Site

Tearaght Island Bird Site

CASTLEMAINE

N22

N23

CASTLEISLAND

Lough Yganavan Natterjack Toad

N22

Lough Nambrackdarrig

KILLARNEY

GLENBEIGH

Dunloe Ogham stones

Muckross friary

Killarney National Park

Sheheree Raised Bog

CAHIRCIVEEN

Eirk Bog Blanket Bog

Derrycunihy Wood Oak Woodland

SOUTH KERRY

KENMARE

N70

Puffin Island Bird Site

SNEEM

Staigue stone fort

N70

N71

Great Skellig

Uragh Wood Woodland

Derrynane

Little Skellig Bird Site

Ilnacullin

GLENGARRIFF

BANTRY

N71

SKIBBEREEN

Lough Hyne Marine Reserve

Knockomagh Woodland

Sherkin Island monastery

CHARLEVILLE

MITCHELSTOWN

N73

KANTURK

Kanturk castle

MALLOW

N72

Labbacallee wedge-tomb

FERMOY

BANTEER

N72

RATHMORE

N20

N8

CORK

MACROOM

The Gearagh Woodland

N22

MIDLETON

N25

COBH

Capel Island Coastal Heathland

N71

DUNMANWAY

BANDON

KINSALE

Ballynacarriga castle

Timoleague abbey

Charles Fort

CLONAKILTY

ROSCARBERY

N71

Old Head of Kinsale Bird Site

stone circle

MILES   10   20   30

KILOMETRES   10   20   30   40   50

National Monuments

CORK

Ballynacarriga/Castle
W29 51

The county of Cork displays a considerable variety in its castles, both Norman and native. The 13th-century example at Liscarroll is one of the largest Norman castles in the country. One of the better native towers of considerably smaller extent is Ballynacarriga, not far from Dunmanway. This four-storey tower-house, prominently sited beside a small stream, may be earlier than the date of 1585 inscribed on a stone on the top floor, which was used as a chapel until 1815.

This top storey bears interesting carvings, including a crucifixion, and the figure of a woman with her three children, accompanied by the letters 'C.C.'. These are perhaps the initials of Catherine Cullinane, wife of Randal Hurley, who may have been the builder of the castle. The tower was protected by a bawn and one of its round bastions still survives.

CORK

Charles Fort/17th-century star-shaped fort
W64 51

The Charles of the Fort at Kinsale is no mere prince, but King Charles II (1660–1685), during whose reign, and in whose honour, the fort was built in the early 1680s by William Robinson, architect of the Royal Hospital in Kilmainham. Kinsale offered a safe haven for the ships which came from many a foreign shore to trade with the town, which was one of the most important in the south of Ireland during the later medieval period.

In the 17th century, two forts were built to protect the town, James Fort on the western bank of the harbour, and Charles Fort on the eastern side, close to the charming village of Summer Cove. This latter is Ireland's most massive fortification. Star-shaped in plan, its walls zigzag in and out in the style devised by Louis XIV's fortification engineer, Vauban, in order to provide cross-fire from a number of directions against any potential aggressor. King Charles's ill-fated successor, James II, occupied the fort with his troops in 1690 but after James's flight from the country his Williamaite opponents exploited the fort's one weak point by firing down upon it from the high ground behind it — and succeeded in taking it. That was the last action the fort ever saw, though it continued to be strengthened and altered, with the addition of many interior barrack buildings, during the subsequent centuries that it remained in military service — until the British troops withdrew in 1921.

Since 1973, the Office of Public Works has carried out extensive repair- and conservation-work to make Charles Fort into one of the most monumental tourist attractions in the whole of Co. Cork.

Open Tuesday to Saturday mid-April to mid-June 9.00–17.00 hours. Sunday 14.00–17.00 hours. Open daily mid-June to mid-September 10.00–18.30 hours.
Enquiries phone (021) 772263.
Literature available at site.

Charles Fort

Kanturk Castle

Drombeg Stone Circle

CORK

Drombeg/stone circle
W26 35

Those parts of Ireland with considerable numbers of stone circles include West Cork, where Drombeg is one of the best known. It consisted of severteen stones making up a ring with a diameter of 9.14 m. One of the stones is recumbent, that is lying down rather than standing, and a line through this stone and the entrance if continued, points to where the sun sets at the winter solstice. However, as only two stones would have been needed to mark this spot on the horizon, the whole circle must have been more than a simple observation point, and its round shape may have connected it somehow with worship of the sun-orb.

One of the two burials, discovered during excavations at the centre of the ring, provided a radiocarbon date within 150 years or so of the time of Christ. But the burial may have been inserted centuries, if not millennia, after the circle had been constructed, as other examples suggest a date during the Bronze Age, from about 2000 BC onwards.

In the same field are two huts of around AD 2nd or 3rd century and another 'stone circle' which turned out, on excavation, to be a *fulachta fiadha*, or ancient cooking place, used somewhat before AD 500.

CORK

Kanturk/Castle
W38 02

On the fringe of the north Cork town of Kanturk stands an interesting example of early 17th-century castle architecture, rectangular in shape but with massive towers at each of the four corners. Its openings combine more traditional Irish styles with the latest manorial style of the Elizabethan period, with a pointed doorway on the ground floor, and a Renaissance door on the first floor of the north side; flattish windows on the

Labbacallee Wedge-Tomb

ground floor, and mullioned Tudor windows in the floors above. Among the interior fittings, pride of place must go to the interesting collection of fireplaces.

The castle was built by Dermod Mac Owen Mac Donagh in 1601, but may never have been completed — either because the English Privy Council, unhappy that such a strong fortress should be in Irish hands, ordered construction to cease, or because Mac Donagh could borrow no more money to complete the building after the news became known of the English victory at the Battle of Kinsale.

CORK

Labbacallee/wedge-tomb
R78 02

Folklore saw in this imposing monument the bed of a hag or witch, but more prosaic and down-to-earth archaeologists see it as the most gigantic example of a type of megalithic wedge-tomb which was common in the southern half of Ireland around 2000 BC. The epithet 'wedge' comes from the wedge-shaped plan of the tomb — the tomb

itself being covered by three heavy capstones. The largest of these measures a massive 7.92 m × 2.43 m. The whole may well have been originally covered by a mound of earth delimited by a series of kerb-stones which, when seen from the side away from the road, makes the tomb look like a prehistoric centipede slowly rising from the ground.

Excavations carried out in 1934 revealed cremated bones, the inhumed remains of one adult male, one child and the body of a headless female, to whom a separate skull found beside that of the adult male may have belonged. She may not have been the hag of the folklore, which gives the tomb its Irish name, but the discovery does support the notion that her body may have lain exposed elsewhere before being interred here.

CORK

Sherkin Island/Franciscan monastery
W03 26

A monastery was founded in 1460 or 1470 by Florence or Dermot O'Driscoll on Sherkin Island in Baltimore Bay, for the Franciscan friars. The church consists of nave, chancel and south transept with two side chapels, and it has a crossing tower which was added in the 16th century. The domestic buildings on the east and west sides of the cloister area still survive, though the cloister arcade itself has disappeared.

The 16th-century building was made necessary as a result of an attack of raiders from Waterford in 1537, when they seized the nearby Dunalong Castle, ravaged the island villages and the friary, setting fire to it. This was to avenge the plundering by the O'Driscolls of a Waterford ship which took refuge in Baltimore during a storm.

Though vacated by the friars at the time of the Dissolution of the Monasteries, the friars returned for some time, *c.* 1637.

CORK

Timoleague/abbey
W47 44

The peaceful inlet where the Argideen River enters Courtmacsherry Bay is dominated by the 13th- or 14th-century 'abbey' of Timoleague, which derives its name Tigh Mo-Laga from a much earlier house founded somewhere in the vicinity by the venerable 7th-century Cork saint, Mo-Laga. The

'abbey' is more correctly a friary, founded by the Franciscans before 1316 by either the MacCarthy Riabhach, or William Barry, both of whom lie buried in the church.

The earliest part of the church is the chancel at the east end, built probably in the 14th century, but much of the remainder belongs to various building stages, all executed in a severely plain style in keeping with the spirit of the friars.

The latest section is probably the graceful tower, added around 1500 by Edmond de Courcy, a Franciscan Bishop of Ross, who is also known to have built a dormitory, an infirmary and a library.

The claustral buildings are quite well-preserved, but the purpose for each individual room is not always easy to work out. In the later 16th and early 17th centuries, the friary was denuded of many of its fittings — and of its friars as well.

KERRY

The Dingle Peninsula/various monuments
Q45 02

The northernmost of the five fingers which project out into the Atlantic Ocean from the south-west of Ireland is the Dingle Peninsula, which preserves a vast number of Christian monuments whose

Sherkin Friary

Reask Stone, Dingle Peninsula

Gallarus Oratory, Dingle Peninsula

Ogham Stone, Dunloe

origin, date and, even use, are often shrouded in mystery. They are, however, probably best understood in conjunction with the pilgrimage traffic to the summit of the peninsula's most famous landmark — Mount Brandon (964.37 m high). The peak was approached from various locations, where a number of beehive huts (pilgrim shelters?) are still preserved, as at Glenfahan. At Reask, excavated in the 1970s, there are two sets of double huts, along with a number of decorated stones, some *in situ,* others displayed in the Heritage Centre at Ballyferriter nearby.

Parts of the old pilgrimage road have recently been repaired, and perhaps the most important stopping-point along its route is the Romanesque nave-and-chancel church at Kilmalkedar, where there is also a sun-dial, an 'alphabet stone', a cross and an Ogham stone.

Close to it is St Brendan's House, probably the
only rural two-storey medieval dwelling to have
survived in Ireland, and a number of boat-shaped
oratories built probably between the 9th and the
12th centuries, of which that at Gallarus — 'the
shelter of the foreigners' — is undoubtedly the best
known.

KERRY

Dunloe/Ogham stones
V88 91

There is no location in the country where Ogham
stones are displayed to better advantage than at
the roadside site at Dunloe, not far from Killarney.
Here a total of seven such stones form a semi-
circle, all of them having been taken from the roof
of a souterrain or underground chamber
discovered at Coolmagort nearby in 1838, while an
eighth, recumbent stone at the centre, was brought
from the church at Kilbonane.

Ogham is an alphabet or cipher of twenty
letters, which are usually formed of groups of
between one and five notches, placed horizontally
on either side of, diagonally across, or at the angle
of, a corner of an upright stone. The inscriptions
at Dunloe are typical in that they record the name
of a person, often giving the name of his father
and/or some remoter ancestor. The person's name
is usually in the genitive case, so that the reader
had to presume the inscription to have been
preceded by some unexpressed formula, such as
'This is the stone of . . .'. Co. Kerry preserves a
great number of these stones, but they are also
found particularly in other Munster counties
bordering the south coast. Others are, however,
found as far away as Wales and Scotland. Some
may be pre-Christian, but the majority probably
date from Christian times up to around the 9th
century, though their original commemorative
purpose remains obscure.

KERRY

Muckross/Franciscan friary
V98 87

The life of the average Franciscan friar in the later
Middle Ages was no bed of roses — nor was it, of
course, meant to be. But for those who had
entered the Friary of Muckross near Killarney, the
way of life must have seemed much more
attractive given the friary's location in the
incomparable setting of the Lakes of Killarney, in
what is now Killarney National Park (see p. 67
below).

The friary was founded for the Franciscans of
the Observantine reform, probably around 1448,
by Donald MacCarthy, and the church and

Muckross Abbey

conventual buildings probably took about twenty-five years to complete. They are remarkably well-preserved, and present us with one of the most outstanding examples of Irish Franciscan architecture of the 15th-century. The church is of the usual friary type, consisting of a long hall, with the slightly later addition of a tower almost exactly half way along its length.

The friary's best-known feature is the fine cloister, the quality of which is in no way diminished by the famous yew-tree growing in the middle of it. The slightly melancholic aspect which the tree creates helps to remind us of the illustrious Kerry chieftains — the MacCarthys, O'Sullivans and O'Donohues — who lie buried within the friary's walls, along with three of the county's most celebrated Gaelic poets of the 17th and 18th centuries: Gothfraidh Ó Donnchadha of the Glen, Aodhagán Ó Rathaille and Eoghan Rua Ó Súilleabháin.

KERRY

Staigue/stone fort
V61 63

A peaceful valley looking towards the sea on the southern side of the Iveragh Peninsula has nestling within it one of the most remarkable stone forts of early Ireland — Staigue Fort on the Ring of Kerry. The sloped stone wall, built without any apparent use of mortar, is up to 5.49 m high and, in places 4 m thick, and it encloses a round area 27.76 m in diameter.

The interior of this wall has 'X'-shaped stairways, facilitating easy access to the top in times of danger. Inside there are also two small chambers within the wall. Outside, there is a large bank and ditch, presumably to make approach more difficult for potential attackers. Inside, the fort is empty, but we must presume the former existence there of houses made of wood, possibly built by some local chieftain who had entrenched himself in the valley, but history is silent as to who he may have been, or when he may have lived.

Staigue Fort

National Parks and Gardens

CORK

Ilnacullin
V94 55

Ilnacullin has an international reputation as an island-garden of rare beauty, located on a fifteen hectare island in Bantry Bay, near Glengarriff.

The central feature of Ilnacullin is a formal Italian-style garden, comprising a rectangular lily-pond surrounded by paved walks, with classical pavilions — the Casita and the Medici House — at each end. The formal garden is set in the midst of wild gardens planted with beautiful trees and shrubs from all continents, including many from South America, Australia, New Zealand, China and Japan. Very mild winters and well-developed shelter belts of conifers combine to favour many tender plants usually associated with warmer climates. Grassy glades and stone steps provide part of a route around the gardens from which to appreciate the form and colour of the plant collections — continuously changing with the seasons.

Eighty years ago the island was windswept and almost barren. It was bought by Annan Bryce who commissioned Harold Peto, one of the leading landscape architects of his time, to design the gardens. In 1953 the island was bequeathed to the State by Bryce's son, Rowland. Sometimes called Garinish Island, the alternative name, Ilnacullin, is now preferred to avoid confusion with another island-garden in Co. Kerry also called Garinish.

Ilnacullin, reached from Glengarriff by a short journey in privately operated boats, is not just attractive as a garden. Other attractions include a Martello Tower, built shortly after 1800, and seals basking on the rocky shores. There are also very fine views of the mountain scenery of West Cork.

Open Monday to Saturday July and August 9.30–18.30 hours. Last landing 17.30 hours. Sunday 11.00–18.00 hours. Last landing 17.30 hours. Monday to Saturday March and October 10.00–16.30 hours. Last landing 16.00 hours. Sunday 13.00–17.00 hours. Last landing 16.30 hours. Monday to Saturday April, May, June and September 10.00–18.30 hours. Last landing 17.30 hours. Sunday 13.00–18.00 hours. Last landing 17.30 hours.
Enquiries phone (027) 63040.
Literature available at site.

KERRY

Derrynane
V53 59

Derrynane at Caherdaniel on the coast of Kerry, was the ancestral home of Daniel O'Connell (1775–1847), lawyer, politician and statesman and one of the greatest figures in Irish history. As his childhood home and his country residence throughout his career, Derrynane had a great influence on his life. The oldest part of the house, inherited by him in 1825, no longer survives, and most of the house as seen today was built to his directions. The house, for long known as Derrynane Abbey, remained in the family for more than a century after Daniel O'Connell's death and in 1967 it was opened to the public as a museum commemorating him.

The Happy Valley, Ilnacullin

Italian Garden, Ilnacullin

Abutilon in flower, Ilnacullin

Derrynane from the air

Ogham stone, Derrynane

Drawing-room, Derrynane

66

The spacious diningroom and drawing-room are decorated in period-style, and retain much of the original furniture, along with a fine collection of family portraits. These rooms, as well as the study and the library, house a fascinating variety of items owned by, or associated with, Daniel O'Connell, and are mementos of his life and times. The chapel was added by him in 1844.

The 130 hectare estate which, together with the house, forms the National Historic Park has many attractions for visitors today. In contrast to most of the surrounding countryside the house is set among trees. Frost-sensitive shrubs are among those flourishing in the sheltered gardens behind the house where there are pleasant walks. A summer house where Daniel O'Connell often worked and a stone cashel are nearby. The park has about a mile of shoreline, including a long sandy beach backed by sand dunes. A nature trail through the dunes explains their formation, ecology and conservation.

On Abbey Island, reached on foot across the sands, except at very high tides, are the ruins of Ahamore Abbey, burial place of many of the O'Connells. The island is also the habitat of the Kerry lily — a rare plant occurring in Ireland only around Derrynane.

Other features within the park are an Ogham stone and a Mass Rock at Altar Hill beside the dunes.

House open Tuesday to Sunday October to April 13.00–17.00 hours. Closed Monday.
Open Monday to Saturday May to September 9.00–18.00 hours. Sunday 11.00–19.00 hours.
Park open during daylight hours.
Enquiries phone (0667) 5113.
Literature available at site

KERRY

Killarney National Park
V98

To the south and west of Killarney town are the world famous Lakes of Killarney. Killarney National Park with its 10,000 hectares comprises the mountains and woodlands which surround these lakes, as well as the three lakes themselves. The park includes the peaks of Mangerton, Torc, Shehy and Purple Mountain, while just to the west rise the MacGillycuddy's Reeks — the highest mountain range in Ireland.

The nucleus of the national park is the 4,000 hectare Bourn Vincent Memorial Park, formerly known as the Muckross estate, which was presented to the State in 1932 by Mr and Mrs W. Bowers Bourn and their son-in-law, Senator Arthur Vincent, to be Ireland's first National Park. In recent years, lands and waters of the former Kenmare estate have been added.

Nature
Within the national park are the most extensive areas of natural woodland remaining in the country. On the sandstone, of which the mountains are composed, are native oakwoods, dominated by oak trees, with an under-storey of holly and other evergreens. There are smaller areas of woodland on limestone, including a yew-wood on the Muckross Peninsula, with the yew-trees growing on almost bare limestone.

The mild oceanic climate permits a luxuriant growth of mosses and filmy ferns, many of them growing as epiphytes on the branches and trunks of the trees. The park also contains interesting bog and moorland vegetation, especially on the uplands.

Some of the characteristic plants of this region are found otherwise only in southern and south-western Europe. Examples are arbutus, St Patrick's cabbage, and greater butterwort.

In the upland areas of the national park, especially on the slopes of Torc and Mangerton, roam the only herd of native red deer remaining in the country. This herd has had a continuous existence since the arrival of red deer in Ireland following the last Ice Age. Introduced Japanese sika deer are found on the open mountain and throughout the woodlands. Most of the other native mammals, as well as long-established introduced species, are to be found in the park.

With the varied habitats of mountain, moorland, woodland and lake the park is rich in bird species. On the uplands the most common birds are meadow pipit, stonechat and raven. Peregrines and merlins are occasionally seen. The woodlands support characteristic bird communities, with chaffinch and robin being the commonest breeders. The lakes are home to heron, mallard, little grebe and water rail, while kingfisher and dipper are frequent on rivers and streams.

In both winter and summer native bird populations are augmented by migrant species. In winter, for example, about 140 Greenland whitefronted geese, of a world population of around 12,000, feed in the Killarney Valley. (See Wildlife, pp. 76, 80).

Natural stocks of brown trout and salmon inhabit the lakes, along with small populations of char, usually a fish of subarctic lakes, and of Killarney shad, a small lake dwelling form of twaite shad.

Centre of Kerry Folk-Life

The focal point of Killarney National Park is Muckross House, completed in 1843 as the residence of the Herbert family. In 1964 the house was opened to the public as a museum of Kerry folk-life, under the management of local Trustees. Since 1980 it has been managed jointly by the Trustees and the Office of Public Works for this purpose and as the principal visitor-centre of the national park.

The principal rooms are furnished in period-style, while much of the house is devoted to folk-life displays, including workshops for craftworkers who demonstrate traditional skills. Other facilities include audio-visual shows and information about the park, a craft shop and a restaurant.

Muckross Gardens

The gardens beside Muckross House are renowned for their fine collection of rhododendrons and azaleas. Large informal expanses of lawn are punctuated by mature Scots pines and large clumps of rhododendron hybrids. There is also a fine rock garden on a natural limestone outcrop, a

Greater butterwort

In the mossy woods, Killarney

*Upper Lake and
Eagle's Nest, Killarney*

formal terrace and sunken garden, a stream garden and ornamental shrub borders. An arboretum, featuring a wide range of less hardy trees and shrubs, was begun in 1972 in a sheltered site adjoining the gardens.

Historic Heritage

The national park is also rich in history and legend from the Bronze Age copper mines of Ross Island to the mythical exploits of the Fianna around Lough Leane up to recent times.

Three major national monuments within the park are of particular interest. On the lake island of Innisfallen are the extensive remains of an early Christian monastery, where the *Annals of Innisfallen*, a major source of information on early Irish history, were completed in the 11th to 13th centuries.

The well-preserved remains of Muckross Abbey,

69

In Muckross House

Romanesque doorway, Innisfallen

a Franciscan friary founded in 1448, were the burial place of chieftains and famous Kerry poets of the 17th and 18th centuries. (See National Monuments, p. 62).

Ross Castle, a 16th-century tower house with a surrounding bawn, was a stronghold of the O'Donoghues, and stands in a beautiful lake-side location. It is currently undergoing structural repairs and restoration.

The landscaped demesnes, which surrounded the homes of the Herberts of Muckross and the Earls of Kenmare, are also part of the national park and provide pleasant walks with fine views of woods, lakes and mountains. Some of the demesne grasslands are grazed by a pedigree herd of black Kerry cattle — now rare, but once the dominant breed in Ireland.

House open daily mid-March to June 9.00–18.00 hours; daily July and August 9.00–19.00 hours; daily September and October 9.00–18.00 hours. Open Monday to Saturday November to mid-March 9.00–18.00 hours. Sundays 11.00–17.00 hours.
Park open during daylight hours.
Enquiries phone (064) 31440.
Literature available at site.

Muckross Gardens

Wildlife

CORK

Capel Island
X29 70

This reserve is part State-, part privately-owned and is located off the south coast near Youghal in Co. Cork. It includes Capel Island itself, Knockadoon Head and an area of sea in between. The island is about 500 m off Knockadoon Head and it was once cultivated, but is now covered by rank growth of grasses. A large colony of herring gulls breed on the cliffs, as do fulmars, shags, great black-backed gulls, cormorants and black guillemots.

The vegetation is also of importance as this is one of the few remaining south coast heath-land sites due to the effects of reclamation elsewhere.

The marine flora and fauna around the island and in the sound are luxuriant.

CORK

Doneraile Park
R61 07

Doneraile Park was formerly the secluded demesne of the St Leger family, Viscount Doneraile, from 1630 to 1969. It is adjacent to the village of Doneraile, which is about five miles north-east of Mallow, and it is open to the public during daylight hours.

Mature groves of deciduous trees, formal tree-lined avenues, vistas and ornamental water areas still reflect the classic 18th-century landscape architecture.

A deer park has existed on this site since the 17th century and deer herds, including native Irish red deer, fallow and sika, are now a special attraction. A network of paths and avenues run through its 160 hectares with car parking, picnic area and a children's playground on site.

Doneraile Court, a classic Georgian mansion, is at present leased to the Irish Georgian Society who have undertaken extensive restoration. Full restoration has yet to be completed.

At the time of writing there are proposals to develop Doneraile Park to a greater level in order to exhibit a wider variety of native fauna, and flora also, in as natural a setting as possible for educational and amenity purposes.

CORK

Knockomagh Wood
W09 28

The wood is situated on a hillside overlooking and adjoining Lough Hyne Nature Reserve. It consists of a small area of native oak and mixed broad-leaved woodland.

It is accessible at all times and there are pathways through the wood.

CORK

Lough Hyne
W10 29

Lough Hyne is situated 6 km south-west of Skibbereen, Co. Cork, and it is Ireland's most important marine nature reserve. It is a sea lough with a very wide range of important habitats.

The reserve contains several thousand species of

Lough Hyne, Co. Cork

marine animals and plants. The fauna and flora of Lough Hyne, The Rapids and Barloge Creek constitute a unique assemblage of marine organisms for an area of only one square kilometre. Situated on the south-west corner of Ireland, the reserve's clean, warm Atlantic water permits survival of southern, or Lusitanian, species of animals and plants, common in the Mediterranean and surrounding areas, together with species peculiar to the rest of Ireland and Britain.

The most noticeable of these southern species at Lough Hyne is the purple sea-urchin [*Paracentrotus lividus*], which occurs in vast numbers along the north shore. The sea-urchin grazes on other species, competing for space on the rocks. Only certain species, such as worms with hard, limy tubes, or hard-shelled molluscs, like the saddle-oyster [*Anomia ephipium*], are able to survive beneath the grazing sea-urchin. It is also possible to observe patches of differently-coloured seabed, corresponding to various intensities of grazing by the species. Heavily-grazed rocks are white with tube-worms and saddle-oysters, while ungrazed areas support dense growths of a variety of other species, including seaweeds.

(**Note:** Bathers should avoid contact with sea-urchins as the spines can prove painful, particularly if stood on, and are brittle and difficult to remove.)

The lough also supports large populations of rare fish, such as couch's goby [*Gobius couchi*] and

Old Head of Kinsale,
Co. Cork

The Gearagh, Co. Cork

the red-mouthed goby [*Gobius cruentatus*], as well as both rare and common species of most groups of marine animals and plants.

At The Rapids a dense forest of the large kelp [*Saccorhiza polyschides*] dominates the narrow tidal channel. Beneath these three, or five, metre-long algae the rocks are emblazoned with coloured sponges, sea-anemones, including the spectacular Jewel anemone [*Corynactic viridis*], fan worms, soft-corals, true corals and sea-squirts. Crawling, or swimming, above this living carpet are predatory worms, molluscs, including multi-coloured sea-slugs, crabs, starfish and fish.

Lough Hyne's vertical underwater cliffs contain a similar profusion of marine life and are acknowledged by scientists and divers alike, for the patchwork beauty of brightly-coloured and curiously-shaped creatures which cover every available square centimetre of rock surface. These beautiful animals and plants are highly sensitive to human disturbance of any kind.

Visitors are requested to avoid trampling on specimens or overturning rocks and are advised to acquaint themselves with the Nature Reserve — Lough Hyne's — Regulations governing its public use.

CORK

Old Head of Kinsale
***W*62 42**

Situated 10 km south of Kinsale, Co. Cork, the Old Head of Kinsale site is of national importance on ornithological and geological grounds. It is a principal breeding site for guillemots and kittiwakes.

Access is possible on foot, but only by pathway along the headland.

CORK

The Gearagh
***W*33 70**

Situated in the middle reaches of the Lee River, just outside of Macroom, Co. Cork, is The

Gearagh, which is the property of the Electricity Supply Board. It is the only extensive alluvial soil forest in Western Europe west of the Rhine and it is unique to the network of woodland nature reserves. It consists of a network of narrow channels separating islands which are covered in oak, ash, birch with a shrub layer of hazel and whitethorn. There are over 100 species of flowering plants and ferns.

From October onwards migratory birds arrive in large flocks. Mallard, wigeon, teal, tufted duck, pochard, great crested grebe, whooper swans, greylag geese, golden plover, dunlin, snipe, curlew and lapwing may be seen on the reservoir and its margins. Several other species of bird may be seen all year round. These include herons, cormorants, coots and moorhens, to name but a few.

The area is marshy, over-grown and exposed to the elements. Visitors may find the region difficult to explore much of the time. It is however possible to walk across the central causeway *when water levels are low,* where much of the bird life can be seen, especially in winter. The roads on the other side can also offer better views of the many birds. The various plant species may be seen from the side-roads around The Gearagh.

At present there is no public access into the wood and it is not advisable to attempt entry due to dangers from the tangle of fallen branches, deep streams, strong currents and soft mud. For the same reasons it is safer to keep to the roads and causeway.

KERRY

Castlemaine Harbour
***V*67 99**

The reserve is situated at the head of Dingle Bay 18 km west of Castlemaine, 20 km east of Dingle and 23 km south-west of Tralee. The area is of international scientific importance on ecological, ornithological and geomorphological grounds. It supports a large colony of brent geese, as well as a large variety of waterfowl.

It is accessible at all times.

Derrycunihy Wood
V89 80

This wood is situated in Killarney valley adjoining and surrounded by Killarney National Park (see p. 67). It is owned by the Irish Forestry Board (Coillte Teo), and it consists of old native oak woodlands with some patches of bog and lakeshore.

Derrymore Island
Q74 11

The island is situated in Tralee Bay, Co. Kerry. It is a compound spit composed of a series of pebble beaches — one of the best examples of its kind in Ireland.

It supports many rare plant communities, mainly of a salt marsh type. The salt marsh on the eastern side of the spit is grazed by wigeon and brent geese. The top of the spit is an important high-tide roosting area for shorebirds.

The island is privately owned and may be viewed from the public roadway only.

Peregrine falcon

Eirk Bog
V85 78

Eirk Bog is situated in the Owenreagh Valley in Killarney 1 km north of Moll's Gap. It is part of a very well-developed and little-disturbed example of an intermediate bog with associated poor fen and blanket bog/wet heath communities.

There is no access to the bog and is best viewed from above on the Killarney/Kenmare road.

Great Skellig
V25 61

Great Skellig is a small precipitous rocky peninsula rising from the Atlantic Ocean approximately 14 km from the mainland of the Iveragh Peninsula in Co. Kerry.

Great Skellig is of international importance for certain seabirds. The most numerous breeding seabirds, apart from Manx shearwaters and storm petrels, are puffins, razorbills and guillemots, kittiwakes and fulmars. The early summer, up to the beginning of July, is the best time to see these birds. It also provides a good example of typical plant communities of small and remote marine islands, including sea campion, sea pink and rock sea spurry, to name but a few.

Little Skellig
V27 62

Little Skellig, like Great Skellig, is also a rocky peninsula of international importance for its gannet breeding colonies — almost 22,000 pairs.

Little Skellig is privately owned and is leased to the Irish Wildbird Conservancy.

The Skelligs are remote rocks and access is difficult even in summer and is normally confined to the purpose of serious research. The gannets circling Little Skellig may be viewed from a boat

Stonechat

Mount Brandon, Co. Kerry

Little Skellig, Co. Kerry

on the way to the larger island, but there are no licensed boats. Strong footwear and waterproofs are advisable.

KERRY

Lough Nambrackdarrig
V70 95

This reserve is situated in the vicinity of Castlemaine Harbour and consists of a fresh water lake, breeding natterjack toads.

Both this and Yganavan reserve may be viewed from the public roadway. There are no visitor services.

KERRY

Lough Yganavan
V70 95

This reserve, like Lough Nambrackdarrig above, is situated in the vicinity of Castlemaine Harbour in Co. Kerry. It is a fresh water lake and is an important breeding site for the natterjack toad, which is Ireland's only toad species.

KERRY

Mount Brandon
Q46 11

The reserve is situated on the north-eastern side of the Dingle Peninsula in Co. Kerry. It consists of

part of the 963-metre high Mount Brandon range of mountains and the foothills. The area is important for the mountain blanket bog/heath complex there and its famed alpine flora.

It is open at all times but is without services. Visitors should use trekking pathways.

KERRY

Puffin Island
V34 67

Puffin Island is situated approximately 500 m off the Iveragh Peninsula in Co. Kerry. It is well-known for its large colonies of breeding seabirds. It is owned by the Irish Wildbird Conservancy.

A marine reserve has been established on the surrounding area of sea and seashore to ensure additional protection for the birds and to control any activities which might cause disturbance.

Access is restricted to serious research purposes and is by prior permission.

KERRY

Sheheree Bog
V98 88

This bog is the only raised bog in the Killarney district of Co. Kerry. It has a well-developed lagg, or marginal drainage system — a very rare feature in this country.

Pyramidal orchids

Grey heron

Puffin Island,
Co. Kerry

Tricoloured pansies

Redshank

It is the habitat of the plant, slender cotton grass, which is protected under the Wildlife Act. The bog is considered to be very valuable for comparative studies with the intermediate and blanket bogs of the Killarney and Owenreagh valleys.

There is no public access to the bog which is privately owned.

KERRY

Tearaght Island
V18 94

Tearaght Island — one of the Blasket group of islands — is of international importance because of the large colonies of seabirds it supports, principally storm petrels and Manx shearwater. A marine reserve has been established on the surrounding area of sea and seashore to ensure additional protection for the birds and to control activities which might cause disturbance.

There is no public access to the island which is privately owned.

KERRY

Tralee Bay
Q74 11

This reserve is situated on the north side of the Dingle Peninsula west of the town of Tralee. It is of international importance for waterfowl, especially the wintering populations of brent geese which it supports.

The reserve is accessible at all times and may be viewed from the public roadway.

KERRY

Uragh Wood
V84 69

Uragh Wood is on the south-west shore of Lough Inchiquin, west of Kenmare, Co. Kerry. It is an excellent example of hyper-oceanic, semi-natural woodland, with native oak being the dominant species.

It is accessible at all times, but there are no visitor services.

Tearaght Island (Inistearaght), Co. Kerry

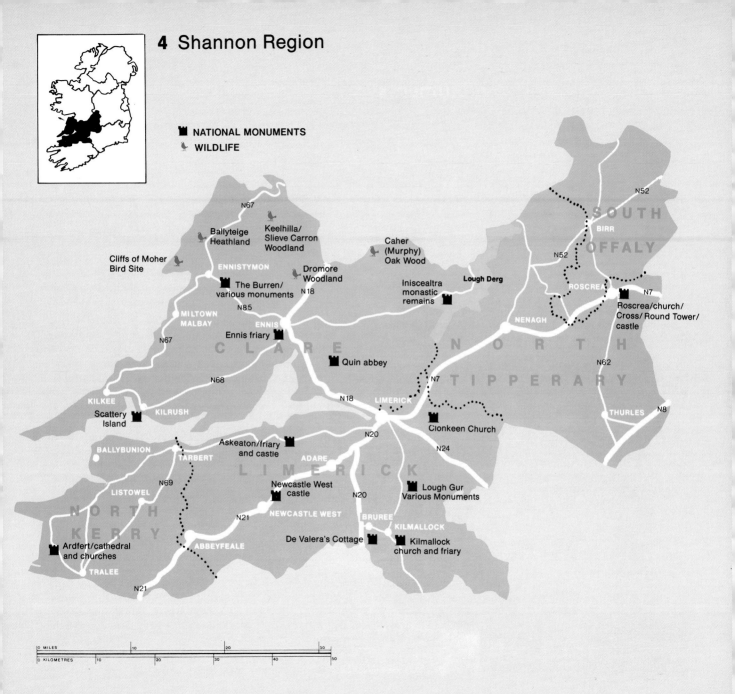

4 Shannon Region

NATIONAL MONUMENTS

WILDLIFE

N67

Ballyteige Heathland

Keelhilla/ Slieve Carron Woodland

Caher (Murphy) Oak Wood

Cliffs of Moher Bird Site

ENNISTYMON

Dromore Woodland

Iniscealtra monastic remains

Lough Derg

The Burren/ various monuments

N18

N52

SOUTH

BIRR

OFFALY

N52

ROSCREA

N62

N85

MILTOWN MALBAY

ENNIS

NENAGH

Roscrea/church/ Cross/ Round Tower/ castle

N7

N67

Ennis friary

C L A R E

N O R T H

Quin abbey

N68

N7

T I P P E R A R Y

THURLES

N8

KILKEE

KILRUSH

LIMERICK

N18

Scattery Island

N20

Clonkeen Church

N24

BALLYBUNION

TARBERT

Askeaton/friary and castle

ADARE

L I M E R I C K

N69

Newcastle West castle

Lough Gur Various Monuments

LISTOWEL

N O R T H

N20

NEWCASTLE WEST

BRUREE

N21

KILMALLOCK

K E R R Y

ABBEYFEALE

De Valera's Cottage

Kilmallock church and friary

Ardfert/cathedral and churches

TRALEE

N21

0 MILES   10   20   30
0 KILOMETRES 10   20   30   40   50

National Monuments

CLARE

The Burren/various monuments
M24 00

It is not surprising that a landscape as unusual and wonderful as the limestone karst of north Clare, known as the Burren, should have produced —and preserved — an equally fascinating collection

Leamaneh Castle, The Burren

not only of flora, but of ancient monuments as well. (See Wildlife p. 92.)

The oldest of these are the megalithic graves — wedge- and portal-tombs — of which Poulnabrone portal-tomb is the best known.

Stone forts, too, abound. One, at Cahercommaun, excavated by American archaeologists in the 1930s, is like an inland Dun Aengus, in using a steep cliff to protect one side, while another fort, Cahermacnaghten, was a famous lawschool down to the 17th century. Almost knitting the forts together is a network of fascinating stone walls, the crooked variety being the more ancient.

The Early Christian sites are among the most attractive, including the diminutive Romanesque Temple Cronán, with its tomb-shrines, hidden away from the road, and the roughly-contemporary churches at Oughtmama.

Kilfenora is famed for having the best collection of 12th-century High Crosses, while Corcomroe Cistercian Abbey, of around 1220, has fine stonework and capitals ornamented with Burren flowers, of the kind presumably grown in the monastery garden for medicinal purposes.

Guarding all of these monuments on the southern end of the Burren is Leamaneh Castle, built in two phases, one of *c.* 1480, the other, dating from the 1640s, built by Conor O'Brien whose wife, Maura Rua, is one of the most famous characters in Clare folklore.

CLARE

Ennis/Franciscan friary
R34 78

The town of Ennis dates the beginning of its 750 years of existence to around 1240, with the foundation of a friary which still remains its most notable feature.

The friary was built for the Franciscans who, together with the Cistercians and Dominicans, were the dominant religious order in medieval Ireland. They were very much an order of, and for, the people, preaching to them and giving them solace, particularly after the grim years of the Black Death which swept across Europe in 1348–50. Indeed, it was the Franciscans above all who were responsible for the revival of church architecture after this disastrous event, particularly in the west of Ireland.

Some of this history is reflected in the structure

Romanesque doorway,
Iniscealtra Island

of Ennis friary, founded by the O'Brien family
who ruled the area for centuries. It was one of
their kings, Turloch, who died in 1306 who gave
the friary much of its present outline — the long
hall-like preachers' church, where all eyes were
once turned towards the five-light east window,
originally resplendent with coloured glass. The
dominant square tower was heightened in the 15th
century, at which time the partially-rebuilt cloister
was also added.

At the foot of the tower is a fine carving of St.
Francis showing his stigmata, and the fine
sculptured panels in the chancel formed part of a
MacMahon tomb of *c.* 1470.

Open daily mid-June to mid-September 10.00–
18.00 hours.
Enquiries phone (065) 29100.
Literature available at site.

CLARE

Iniscealtra/monastic remains
*R*69 85

The peaceful island of Iniscealtra, otherwise
known as Holy Island, lies in an arm of Lough
Derg on the lower Shannon, reachable by boat
from near Mountshannon. Its monastic origins are
associated with three saints: the fabulous
MacCreiche, St Colm of Terryglass (on the
Tipperary mainland opposite) and Caimin. It is
with the last-named that the major church on the
island is associated, with its inserted Romanesque
doorway reconstructed from fragments found
during excavation.

It houses parts of three High Crosses. Nearby is
a Round Tower, perhaps never completed, and a
curious structure known as 'The Confessional',
which may have marked St Caimin's grave.

There are two other churches on the island, the

'Baptism Church' with a 12th-century doorway, and the larger 13th-century St Mary's. In addition, the island has a large collection of cross-decorated slabs, second only in extent to that at Clonmacnois. The monastery may have come to an end around 1200, but for centuries afterwards, Iniscealtra was a centre of Whitsuntide pilgrimage.

CLARE

Quin/abbey
R42 74

Quin 'abbey' is a curious admixture of two contrasting and ill-matched monuments, representing a see-saw battle between the temporal and spiritual powers of medieval Ireland. The basis is a square castle built by the Norman Thomas de Clare in the 13th century, the round bastions of which can still clearly be seen. It was sacked by the Irish in 1286, and it was almost exactly a century and a half later, in 1433, that Síoda Cam Macnamara — of the same family who were responsible for the building of Bunratty Castle — erected on the ruins of the castle a noble friary for the Franciscan friars.

This friary, with a church having a fine east window, a tower and a south transept, also has one of the best-preserved Franciscan cloisters in the country, with dormitories on the first floor. The tall building, its height emphasised by the tower, seems to rise like a phoenix above the ashes of the Norman castle, and it must surely have been seen as a symbol of the resurgence of Gaelic Ireland after Norman power in Clare had been shattered in the Battle of Dysert O'Dea in 1318.

CLARE

Scattery Island/monastic remains
Q97 52

The 36.58 m high Round Tower of Scattery Island is among the tallest and most prominent landmarks in the lower reaches of the Shannon Estuary. It marks the site of a monastery founded by one of Co. Clare's best-known early saints, St

Quinn Friary

Aughnanure Castle (see p. 96)

Senan, in the 6th century on an island called after a monster, Cata, which the saint is said to have slain with some assistance from an angel. The well-preserved Round Tower is unique in Ireland in having its doorway at ground level, a feature which made access to it all too easy when the Vikings attacked — and possibly even occupied — the island in the 9th and 10th centuries. It was later won back by Brian Boru, the Clare-born victor of the Battle of Clontarf.

The other buildings on the island are churches, one with antae — walls protruding beyond the gables — another being a Romanesque nave-and-chancel structure, a third called the Church of the Hill of the Angel — the one which helped St Senan overcome the monster — and finally the Church of the Dead, near the landing place. These buildings underwent alterations and reconstructions during the later medieval period,

Round Tower and Cathedral, Scattery Island

when the island suffered depredations from the Normans.

LIMERICK
_____

Askeaton/friary and castle
R34 50

Even the most disinterested motorist travelling along the new road by-passing the west Limerick village of Askeaton cannot fail to be struck by the remains of the Franciscan friary which now abuts it. The friary was founded for the Franciscans probably by Gerald 'The Poet', 4th Earl of Desmond, in 1389, though the buildings date largely from the period 1420–40.

In the same way that its founder heralded a re-birth of native Gaelic poetry, the friary is one of the earliest buildings to show the revival of monumental architecture and sculpture after the country had been devastated by the effects of the Black Death in 1348–50. Significantly, it was in the west that this revival started, giving a lead which was followed only some time later in the east of the country. Perhaps the friary's most notable feature is the well-preserved cloister, bearing at its north-eastern corner a carving of the order's founder showing his stigmata.

Not far away, on the other side of the bridge over the River Deal, is a Norman castle, founded on an island around 1190, probably by William de Burgo.

LIMERICK
_____

Clonkeen Church
R69 55

This small Romanesque church, situated in a picturesque churchyard, is a simple rectangular church with antae, of a typical 12th-century form. It is best known for its fine sandstone doorway, which has a hood with incised decoration of chevrons, beads and dentils, and animal heads at each end. A head also decorates the top of the arch. The arch is supported by almost full

Dominican Friary, Kilmallock

octagonal pillars with bulbous capitals and decorated square bases. The doorway was subject to early vandalism — initials carved on it in 1779 are still clearly visible. The church has a 12th-century round-headed window in the north wall, and also has two inserted 15th-century windows at the east.

Little is known of its history. The patron of the church was Diommog or Little Diomma venerated on 26 April. Clonkeen [Ir. *Cluain Caoin,* beautiful meadow] was mentioned in the *Annals of the Four Masters,* when a plundering expedition went by river as far as Clonkeen, raiding cattle and carrying off captives.

LIMERICK

De Valera's Cottage
R55 30

In the late 19th century, many cottages were built by local authorities to house labourers or farm workers. The cottage in Bruree, in which Eamon de Valera grew up, was built by the Kilmallock

Union in about 1880, to a standard design. The young Eamon de Valera came from New York to live with his grandmother, Mrs Coll, in 1885, and went to the local school. In 1898 he left Bruree for Dublin at the age of sixteen.

The cottage was altered during its occupation, retaining the basic accommodation of a kitchen and two other rooms downstairs, with an upper floor of two bedrooms. The kitchen still has its machine bellows by the fire.

During renovation by the Office of Public Works, the original colour of the house was uncovered and was reused, and the layout of cobbles to the front became evident when later walls were removed.

LIMERICK

Kilmallock/medieval church and friary
R61 28

The town of Kilmallock owes its origin to a monastery founded in the 7th century by St Mo-cheallóg, from whom it gets its name, but it owed its former medieval splendour to the famous

Anglo-Norman family, the Fitzgeralds, who fortified the town in 1375. Its centrepiece was the church of SS Peter and Paul, founded and built in the 13th century, but possibly incorporating an earlier Round Tower, and later altered in the 15th century. It was in the church that the 'Sugán' Earl of Desmond surrendered to the Queen's forces in 1600 and the subsequent attendance at a Protestant service there by James, the 15th Earl, caused many of his subjects to rebel against him.

Reached by a path from St John's Gate, one of the two surviving medieval town gates, is a far finer piece of architecture, the Dominican friary. Founded in 1291, but completed early in the following century by Maurice, the first Fitzgerald White Knight, whose family came to dominate the locality for centuries, the friary is one of the best buildings surviving in the country from the period around 1300, when Norman building activity was already on the wane. The church is not only noted

*Wedge-tomb,
Lough Gur*

for its five-light west window, but also for the quality of its masonry and foliate carving.

LIMERICK

Lough Gur/miscellaneous field monuments
R64 41

Lough Gur, in south-east Limerick, is the largest lake in the county, and it has provided adequate watering and cooling facilities for the herds of cattle grazing on the lush pastures close by, which have attracted settled pastoralists to the area for well-nigh 5,000 years, if not more. It was more than just the small archaeological community which registered delight and amazement in the 1940s when excavations on Knockadoon, a headland jutting into the lake, began to reveal the presence there of the first Stone Age houses to have been found in Ireland. Some of the houses were rectangular in shape, others oval or rounded, and often constructed with a stone foundation and perhaps a thatched roof, though it must be said that not all of them were necessarily lived in at the same time.

The fields around Lough Gur are full of ancient remains of one sort or another. There is a megalithic tomb, Early Christian-period round houses, a number of stone circles and two medieval castles, known as Bourchier's Castle and Black Castle.

The most imposing monument of all is not close to the lake at all, but is that known as the Great Stone Circle in Grange townland, beside the Limerick–Kilmallock road.

LIMERICK

Newcastle West/castle and banqueting halls
R28 33

Newcastle West, historically known as Newcastle in Oconyll, lies in the fertile plains of west Limerick, almost close enough to protect the pass across the hills to Kerry. It was the chief manor of the Desmond Geraldines, and it was probably a member of this great Anglo-Norman family, Thomas Fitzmaurice — known as 'The Ape', for having been brought to the top of a tower and safely down again by an ape — who founded the new castle around the late 13th century, without our knowing too much about any previous 'old castle' which may have preceded it.

With the new castle, the Geraldines sealed their grip on the surrounding land, which they held until the castle was surrendered to the English in 1569. At that period, the castle is known to have been square in shape with a round tower at each corner, and also including a peel tower and probably two halls, as well as orchards, gardens and its own fish pond. What are probably the two halls (one close to the town square, the other near an adjacent river), as well as the peel tower and a part of the curtain wall, is all that now survives, probably dating in large part to the restoration works carried out by James, Earl of Desmond, in the first half of the 15th century.

Having only been taken into the care of the Office of Public Works in recent times, a programme of conservation works is *en train* which will make the much-neglected remains of this fine castle more widely appreciated by the general public.

TIPPERARY

Roscrea/church/Cross/Round Tower/castle
S14 89

The road from Dublin to Limerick cuts through the centre of the old monastery of Roscrea, which St. Crónán founded early in the 7th century after his earlier monastery at Sean Ros had become too small to house the great number of his disciples.

Immediately beside the road is the surviving west wall of a fine 12th-century church, with its blind arcades flanking the doorway which contains a figure (presumably St. Crónán) in its gable. Close by is a much-pitted 12th-century High Cross with figures in high relief of Christ and,

presumably again, St. Crónán. In its pristine state this cross must have been one of the finest of its period in Ireland.

On the opposite of the road is a Round Tower, with a curious carving of a medieval boat on the inside of one of its upper windows. In the 13th century, the ancient monastery was eclipsed by the construction, only a hundred yards away, of a strong Norman castle.

The early 18th-century Damer House,* in which is located Roscrea Heritage Centre, stands in the castle courtyard.

*Not in the care of the Office of Public Works.

KERRY

Ardfert/cathedral and churches
Q79 21

A number of interesting churches still bear testimony to Ardfert being once the most important medieval town in Co. Kerry. It centred around the cathedral, which owed its importance to the cult of the famous navigator, St. Brendan, who was born here around 484, and who voyaged with a small band of men across the Atlantic waves to Iceland and probably to Greenland, possibly even as far as America.

The earliest part of the building is the western end with its Romanesque doorway and blind-arcading with net-like masonry — based, perhaps, on a French model. It was subsequently extended to its present elongated size in the 13th century. Nearby is an Ogham stone and two smaller churches, the decorative 12th-century Temple na Hoe and the 15th-century Temple na Griffin, which gets its name from a carving beside a window in the interior north wall.

Almost a mile away, to the east, is a well-preserved Franciscan friary founded around 1253 by Thomas Fitzmaurice, though the south transept and the cloisters are a 15th-century addition.

Wildlife

CLARE

Ballyteige
R15 97

This is a reserve situated 2 km west of Lisdoonvarna in Co. Clare. It consists of five parcels of wet meadow and heath. These are being managed in the traditional way for hay-making with the objective of maintaining them as examples of the wet meadow found over the shale soils of the region.

It is accessible at all times and it can be viewed from the adjoining public roadway.

Shelduck

CLARE

Caher (Murphy)
R57 92

Caher Murphy is in the Slieve Aughty Mountains range, Co. Clare. It is an area of oak wood on moist fertile soil and contains a rich ground flora.

CLARE

Cliffs of Moher
R03 91

The Cliffs of Moher extend for some 7 km and are more or less vertical along most of their expanse. Their height varies between 90 m and 200 m.

The cliff face is composed of horizontally-layered flagstones which form ideal nesting sites for seabirds. These include fulmars, kittiwakes, razorbills, guillemots and puffins. Other birds include shags, great black-backed and herring gulls, peregrines, ravens, and choughs.

There is a rough pathway along much of the cliffs' edge and visitors may use this but should exercise caution because of the steepness of these cliffs.

The area has visitor services with a restaurant and a small interpretative centre which are open during the main tourist season.

CLARE

Dromore
R35 85

This reserve consists of a semi-natural woodland with major wetland types and it is situated 10 km north of Ennis.

Merlins

Hen harrier

Meadow pipit

Sandwich terns

The area is particularly valuable for its variety of habitats. These include hazel and ash scrub which are characteristic of carboniferous limestone outcrops. It is especially valuable as a habitat for one of our rarest mammals — the pine marten. Other habitats include limestone pavement, lakes, lakeshore communities, wet grassland subject to flooding, fen, dry limestone grassland, oakwoods and alder/willow carr.

This area is readily accessible with a road network and parking facilities.

CLARE

Keelhilla, Slieve Carron
M32 03

This reserve is situated at the north-eastern edge of the Burren plateau in Co. Clare. It is a good example of karst topography (see National Monuments, p. 82), containing three distinctive vegetation communities: woodland, scrub grassland and pavement.

It is accessible at all times and there are car-parking facilities near the site.

OFFALY

Mongan Bog
N03 30

The bog is situated 2 km east of Clonmacnois, Co. Offaly. It is between two esker ridges and has well-developed pools and hummocks. It is a feeding/roosting site for Greenland white-fronted geese.

The area is unsafe for the general public. It is owned by An Taisce from whom permission should be sought to visit it for serious research purposes only.

*Cliffs of Moher
Co. Clare*

Willow warbler

Chough

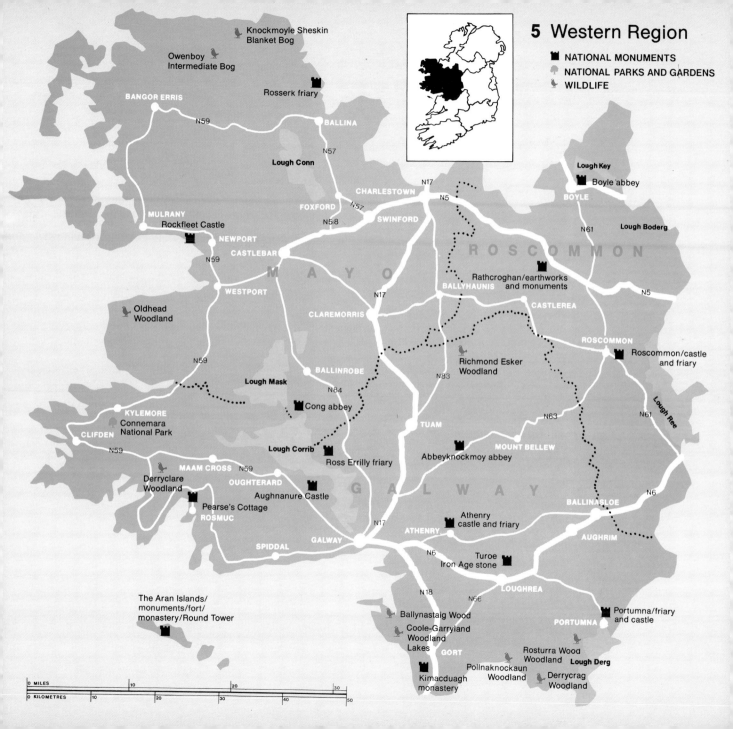

5 Western Region

- ■ NATIONAL MONUMENTS
- ♣ NATIONAL PARKS AND GARDENS
- 🐦 WILDLIFE

Knockmoyle Sheskin
Blanket Bog

Owenboy
Intermediate Bog

Rosserk friary

BANGOR ERRIS

N59

BALLINA

N57

Lough Conn

CHARLESTOWN

N17

N5

Lough Key

Boyle abbey

BOYLE

N61

Lough Boderg

FOXFORD

N57

SWINFORD

ROSCOMMON

MULRANY

Rockfleet Castle

NEWPORT

CASTLEBAR

N58

MAYO

N59

WESTPORT

N17

BALLYHAUNIS

Rathcroghan/earthworks
and monuments

CASTLEREA

N5

Oldhead
Woodland

CLAREMORRIS

Richmond Esker
Woodland

ROSCOMMON

Roscommon/castle
and friary

N59

N83

Lough Ree

N61

BALLINROBE

Lough Mask

N84

TUAM

N63

Cong abbey

KYLEMORE

Connemara
National Park

CLIFDEN

Lough Corrib

Ross Errilly friary

Abbeyknockmoy abbey

MOUNT BELLEW

N59

MAAM CROSS

N59

Derryclare
Woodland

OUGHTERARD

Aughnanure Castle

GALWAY

BALLINASLOE

N6

Pearse's Cottage

ROSMUC

Athenry
castle and friary

SPIDDAL

GALWAY

ATHENRY

AUGHRIM

N17

N6

Turoe
Iron Age stone

LOUGHREA

The Aran Islands/
monuments/fort/
monastery/Round Tower

N18

N66

Ballynastaig Wood

Coole-Garryland
Woodland
Lakes

GORT

Portumna/friary
and castle

PORTUMNA

Rosturra Wood
Woodland

Lough Derg

Pollnaknockaun
Woodland

Derrycrag
Woodland

Kimacduagh
monastery

0 MILES   10   20   30
0 KILOMETRES   10   20   30   40   50

National Monuments

Abbeyknockmoy/Cistercian abbey
M 51 44

We owe to the Cistercians some of the finest medieval churches surviving in Ireland. One of these imposes itself strongly on the gently-undulating, if sometimes bleak, limestone landscape of east Galway in the shape of Abbeyknockmoy.

The abbey was founded around 1190 by Cathal Crovdearg O'Conor, King of Connacht, who was buried there, as were many of his family. It was colonised from Boyle, that other great Cistercian outpost in the west. The monks may have been on the site for about twenty years before they started building, for the style of architecture makes the church unlikely to be earlier than about 1210.

It has the characteristic cross-shaped plan, with the finest masonry in the eastern part, consisting of the presbytery or chancel with fine ribbed vaulting, and two transepts, each with two side-chapels. The nave was blocked off in the later medieval period. It is in the chancel that the most unusual feature of the abbey is to be found: the recently restored line-painting — not a fresco as it is usually called — depicting the Crucifixion, the medieval legend of the Three Dead and the Three Living Kings, and the martyrdom of St Sebastian pierced with arrows when tied to the trunk of a tree.

Recent excavations have revealed traces of the cloister, which was added around 1500, at the same time that the once-fine chapter house, with triple lancet windows in the adjoining east wing of the conventual buildings, was barbarously subdivided into three sections.

The Aran Islands/monuments/fort/monastery/Round Tower
L 76–99 00–13

The three Aran islands of Inishmore, Inishmaan and Inisheer — the large, middle and eastern islands respectively — lie like three jewels in the crown of Galway Bay, sparkling with a great richness and variety of ancient monuments, pagan and Christian.

The most dramatic of these monuments is Dun Aengus, a series of semi-circular fortifications perched on a cliff-edge falling 60.97 m sheer into the Atlantic below which, of course, saved the builders from having to construct the other half. According to legend, it and another, almost equally notable rounded stone fort, were built by the Fir Bolg, a tribe related to the Belgae whom Caesar overcame in Gaul, and who dug themselves into island life here after they were banished from Co. Meath for having refused to pay their taxes to a local king.

Scarcely had the historic period dawned when the stony fields of Aran played host to an immigrant of a different kind — St Enda, who sought refuge from the world, and who settled at Killeany to found a monastery which reaped a harvest one hundredfold, in being the 'nursery' which trained many of the founders of the great monasteries of early Christian Ireland.

Signs of early sanctity on the islands are found

Dun Conor Fort, Inishmaan.

in the many churches, a Round Tower and 12th-century crosses. Though it has never been proved, it is possible that the fragmentary condition of these crosses may be due to the iconoclastic activities of the Cromwellians who built Arkin's Castle on Inishmore.

GALWAY

Athenry/castle/friary
M50 28

Athenry is one of the most notably Norman towns in Co. Galway, owing its foundation to Meiler de Bermingham, who had been granted much of Connacht when the Normans overran it in 1235. De Bermingham was not long in erecting a great three-storey keep, or tower, in his new centre of power at Athenry. For safety reasons, it was

Temple Mac Duagh, Inishmore

entered at first-floor level through a doorway, which, however, is decorated on the outside with plant-decorated capitals — an unexpectedly elegant touch in a fortress designed to withhold attacks from the native Irish.

One such attack took place outside the castle in 1316; it almost succeeded, and the proceeds of the victory went to build new town walls which, with their round bastions and a town gate, still remain partially intact. The keep itself was surrounded by a smaller version of these walls, and recent excavations within have brought to light foundations of other buildings of various dates.

Not far away is a De Bermingham foundation of another kind — the Dominican friary of SS Peter and Paul, though some of its monastic buildings were the result of native Irish patronage. Founded in 1241, the church was extended in the 14th century with the addition of a north aisle and transept with splendid window, and recently-restored archway beneath. The town also contains other medieval traces,* including a fragment of a 15th-century Market Cross carved with a crucifixion — the only medieval Market Cross to survive in anything approximating to its original position in Ireland.

*Not in the care of the Office of Public Works.

GALWAY

Aughnanure/Castle
M15 42

Aughnanure Castle, perched on a small limestone plateau, provides a pretty picture when reflected in the calm waters of a stream emerging from a rock-bridge which gives access to the castle. The tower was built in the 16th-century by the O'Flaherty family, who protected it outside with two bawns, the inner one with an elegant corbel-roofed angle-turret and the outer one with a fine banqueting hall. But only one wall of the banqueting hall survives, as the remaining parts disappeared centuries ago when the ground on which it stood

Round Tower and Cathedral, Kilmacduagh

collapsed into the underground river beneath.

Although the citizens of Galway erected the west gate of their city to protect themselves from 'the ferocious O'Flaherties', it was, paradoxically, this O'Flaherty castle which acted as an outpost around upper Lough Corrib, relieving the city during a Cromwellian blockade!

Open daily mid-June to mid-September 10.00–18.00 hours.
Enquiries phone (091) 82214.
Literature available at site.

GALWAY

Kilmacduagh/early monastery
M40 00

Kilmacduagh, close to the border of counties Galway and Clare, stands almost in the shadow of the beautiful limestone hills of the Burren. Because it is somewhat off the beaten track, it tends to be rather unjustly overlooked as one of the most interesting examples of early monastic architecture in the west of Ireland. The name

Portumna Castle

means the church of Mac Duagh, a famous 7th-century saint also commemorated by a church on the Aran Islands. He was a kinsman for a local king, Guaire Aidhne, renowned for his hospitality.

The monastery's most notable feature is the one which first attracts the visitor's attention from a distance, as it did when first erected almost a thousand years ago — the Round Tower, which is probably the best-preserved example in the whole country. Unusually, however, this one leans two feet out of the perpendicular, like its more famous counterpart at Pisa, which was built some centuries after it.

Close by is the simple, roofless cathedral, the blocked-up west doorway of which belongs to the first stone church on the site, which was later extended in the Gothic period. In the fields around can be seen a number of small churches — that on the other side of the road being dedicated to the Virgin, and perhaps reserved for women. But the most attractive church lies a few hundred yards north-west of the cathedral, close to a small lake. This is O'Heyne's church, dating from the early 13th century, built to the north of a small cloister garth, and with excellent masonry in the chancel arch and east window.

Near the car park is the recently-restored Glebe, or Abbot's House, dating from the later medieval period, long after the monastery's heyday had passed.

Portumna/friary and castle
M85 04

The lands at the northern end of Lough Derg, close to the town of Portumna, provide an appropriate setting for two disparate monuments placed close to one another — a Dominican friary and a 17th-century mansion.

The friary got its dedication to SS Peter and Paul from a chapel of the Cistercians from Dunbrody which, on becoming disused, was granted around 1426 to the Dominican friars, who subsequently built the present aisleless church and conventual buildings, probably with the assistance of the local O'Madden chieftain. Noteworthy are the traceried south and east windows, one of them bearing a signature 'Johanne' — a very rare example of an Irish medieval mason signing his work.

By 1582, the friary was in the hands of the Earls of Clanrickarde, and it was Richard, the 4th Earl, who was responsible for the building of the castle, or 'strong-house', nearby. Of an old Anglo-Irish family, his wife and his loyalty to the English crown had led him to spend most of his life in England, and he may not even have been in Ireland when his house was built at Portumna sometime before 1618.

The building is rectangular in shape, with a square turret at each corner, and it has two closely-spaced walls in its long axis, between which lay stairs leading to the upper floors. The castle battlements are a combination of Jacobean-style and medieval Irish crenellations, in the same way that the northern doorcase on the first floor combines the latest classical-style and utilitarian pistol-loops, which show it to be still a fortified house rather than a mansion. The castle is approached by two formal gardens of unequal size, the innermost one having a gateway which is one of the earliest surviving examples of the exterior use of a classical order in Irish architecture.

Rosmuc/Pearse's Cottage
L92 34

Overlooking a stretch of water near Rosmuc in Connemara is a typical thatched house or cottage, one of those native buildings which innately fits so

Pearse's Cottage

snugly and naturally into the Irish landscape. What makes this one so different from many others of its kind is that it was built to serve as the summer home of the poet and patriot, Pádraig Pearse (1879–1916). Here in the locality he was to soak up knowledge of the Irish language, lore and legend, which he put to such good use when teaching in the Irish school he founded at Scoil Éanna/St Enda's in the Dublin suburb of Rathfarnham, which is now a Pearse Museum and is in the care of the Office of Public Works. (See National Parks and Gardens, p. 26.)

This cottage, too, can be described in its own way as a Pearse Museum, for it is simply furnished in the style in which he lived, before going out to face the British firing-squad for his part in the Easter Rising of 1916 — the 'blood sacrifice' which he himself felt was so necessary in order to achieve the independence of Ireland for which he longed so much.

Open daily June to September 10.00–18.00 hours. Literature available at site.

GALWAY

Ross Errilly/Franciscan friary
M25 48

Just on the Galway side of a small stream, which forms the boundary with Co. Mayo on the eastern shores of Lough Corrib, are the exceptionally well-preserved remains of Ross 'abbey'. Founded for the Observantine Franciscans in 1498, the friary was not only one of their last foundations before the Reformation, but also one of the largest — its size being heralded from afar by the extensive zigzag gable skyline of the buildings flanking the tall tower at the centre of the church.

While the church itself is of the usual long hall variety of the friars, it is the presence of not one, but two, courtyards to the north of the church which makes the buildings so extensive. Around them are grouped the domestic buildings, including a refectory with reader's desk, first-floor

dormitories and a kitchen with built-in fish-tank, ante-dating that modern restaurant idea by several centuries!

After the Dissolution of the Monasteries, the friars were protected by the Earls of Clanrickarde, but the English occupied the buildings in 1596, and the Cromwellians pillaged them in 1656, leaving them denuded of both furniture and roof as they are today.

GALWAY

Turoe/Iron Age decorated stone
M62 23

The domed granite pillar, almost 1.22 m high, standing in the grounds of Turoe House not far from the village of Bullaun, is the finest of the four elaborately-carved stones to survive from the pre-Christian Iron Age in Ireland.

Above a frieze of step-pattern, the dome is covered with a composition of flowing curvilinear forms typical of the insular La Tene art style of the prehistoric Celts, suggesting a date for the stone within a century of Christ's birth. The designs which may originally have been heightened by colouring, have been shown to be divided into two unequal pairs of parts, which may have been adapted from some four-sided obelisk-like design.

The stone formerly stood close to a nearby ringfort, called the Rath of Feerwore, or the Fort of the Strong Men, where objects of Iron Age date were excavated in 1938. But what form of cult may have been practised around the stone can now only be left to our imagination.

MAYO

Cong/Augustinian abbey
M14 55

Idyllically situated between Loughs Corrib and Mask, Cong was one of Mayo's earliest monasteries, having probably had St. Feichin of Fore as one of its abbots in the 7th century. The importance of the monastery during the 12th century is demonstrated by its possession of the wonderful processional Cross of Cong — now one of the glories of the National Museum in Dublin.

The Cross was created in the 1120s to house what may have been the first relic of the True Cross to have reached Ireland. It was commissioned by Turlough O'Conor, the High King, who re-founded the abbey with the assistance of the Augustinian Canons. It was his son, Rory, Ireland's last high king, who started the construction of the buildings which still survive today. This was probably around 1200, though building probably continued as late as 1228, when many masons left Connacht because of the hardship caused by O'Conors' wars.

Of the church, only the chancel survives relatively intact, entered from the car-park through a doorway built of stones re-assembled there in 1860, with the financial assistance of Sir Benjamin Lee Guinness, builder of the adjoining castle* in whose estate the monastery lay. Even finer doorways adorn the eastern side of the cloister, superb examples of the masonry and carving executed by the 'School of the West', probably in the 1220s. Other interesting carvings are found on the capitals of the reconstructed cloister, but these are works, not of the 13th century, but of Sir Benjamin's 19th-century mason, Peter Foy.

*Not in the care of the Office of Public Works.

MAYO

Rockfleet/Castle
L93 95

Otherwise known as Carrigahowley, this castle is a quite straightforward 15th- or 16th-century tower-house holding back the waves of Clew Bay, as it were. It is a four-storey structure with a corner turret. What makes it much more interesting is its association with the legendary and romantic pirate queen of the 16th-century, Grace O'Malley, who is

Iron Age La Tène decorated stone, Turoe house

*Rosserk
Franciscan Friary*

alleged not to have bowed in the presence of
Queen Elizabeth I, because she saw her as an
equal.

One of Elizabeth's naval expeditions was sent
from Galway to subdue the castle in 1574, but the
wily Connacht woman successfully repulsed it,
and went to reside permanently in the tower after
the death of her second husband, Sir Richard
Burke, in 1583. One can well imagine her warming
herself and her protectors from the westerly
Atlantic winds in front of the fireplace which is
still preserved on the top floor.

MAYO

Rosserk/Franciscan friary
G25 25

If any of the surviving grey-stoned Franciscan
friaries of medieval Ireland can be described as
'cosy', then it is Rosserk, peacefully situated beside
the shore of Killala Bay. It could merit the epithet
because it is comparatively small and homely, with
attractive 15th-century doorway, delicate tower
and small cloister garth without the usual
ambulatories.

The most interesting feature is the piscina,
through which water was poured away after Mass.

It has two eye-like openings giving a view on to the
sea outside, but what catches the eye are the two,
almost smiling, angels in the spandrels bearing
instruments of Christ's passion — one the flail and
the other the nails. On the left-hand column is
a unique carving of a four-storey Round Tower
on a prism-like base. Rosserk is the only friary
listed in this guide which was built by the Tertiary,
or Third Order, Franciscans who, when founded
originally by St. Francis, consisted of laymen and
women, but subsequently its members were friars
whose rules differed from those of the Conventual
and Observant friars of the order.

The foundation was effected through a member
of the Joyce family by 1441, and its end came in
1596 when it was pillaged by Sir Richard
Bingham, the English Governor of Connacht who,
however, was unable to divest it of that intimate
charm which still comes across to us almost four
centuries after its devastation.

ROSCOMMON

Boyle/Cistercian abbey
G80 03

The Cistercian monks, who so obligingly chose a
location beside the modern Dublin-Sligo road to

build their monastery on the River Boyle in 1161, had come from Mellifont (see page 138) — the first and foremost of all the Cistercian foundations in Ireland. The French church designs which had influenced the plan of Mellifont Church were still sufficiently strong to impress themselves on the earliest, eastern part of the church at Boyle, with its barrel-vaulted chancel, and two chapels to each of the transepts. The remainder of the church took about sixty years to complete, and its various building stages can clearly be seen as the round arch gives way to the pointed in the more western portions. The Romanesque decoration is replaced by capitals and corbels with attractive figures and animals, which seem to flout desire for simplicity and lack of figure carving expressed by the order's most brilliant preacher, St Bernard of Clairvaux.

The conventual buildings have suffered through use as a barracks in the 17th-century, but the first-floor gatehouse on the western side of the cloister has recently been restored, and displays a large-scale model of the monastery and its surrounds.

Open daily mid-June to mid-September 10.00-18.00 hours.
Enquiries phone (079) 62604.
Literature available at site.

ROSCOMMON

Rathcroghan/earthworks and monuments
M80 84

The *Táin Bó Cuailgne's* legendary pillow-scene, in which Queen Maeve discovers that her husband Ailill's herd of cattle had a finer bull than hers, is traditionally located at Rathcroghan between Tulsk and Belanagare, in the windswept plains of Roscommon. It was here, too, that Maeve began to gather her army to go out and fight Cuchulainn and his fellow Ulster warriors. But precisely where all these happenings may have taken place would be difficult to locate more exactly in the midst of the great richness of earthworks at Rathcroghan, including round earthworks, flat-topped mounds, linear earthworks and a souterrain with Ogham

stones which the ancient Irish consider to be one of the entrances to the Underworld.

Some of these monuments have old names associated with them — Relignaree [King's Cemetry], Dathi's mound [after a 5th-century king], Rathnadarbh [Rath of the bulls], but, in fact, we know surprisingly little solid history about this complex of earthworks which stretches over many square miles and doubtless well over a thousand years, on either side of the coming of Christianity. It is imagination which provides the best aid to history when confronted with a rich and baffling array of earthworks such as this!

ROSCOMMON

Roscommon/castle and friary
M88 64-65

Along with Athenry in the neighbouring county of Galway, the town of Roscommon is the proud possessor of medieval remains where castle and church stand in comparatively close proximity to one another. The castle, a vast square building with rounded corner bastions and entry between two turrets in the western wall, was built by the Lord Justice of Ireland, Robert de Ufford, in 1269. But such a stronghold being a prize possession in the days when knights were very bold, ownership of the castle frequently changed — ping-pong-like — between the Irish and the English, and it was the latter, under Sir Nicholas Malby, Governor of Connacht, who gave the castle its present form by transforming one part of it into a fortified Elizabethan manor-house with mullioned windows.

The Dominican friary was, in contrast, an Irish foundation, having been set on its feet by Felim O'Conor, Lord of Roscommon, in 1253, and it is what is alleged to be his effigy which is the building's most interesting feature. It lies in a burial niche in the north wall of the chancel, supported by eight mail-clad warriors [Gallowglasses] who, however, belonged to a different and much later tomb of *c.* 1500.

National Parks and Gardens

GALWAY

Connemara National Park
L75

Situated in the heart of the west of Ireland, Connemara National Park covers some 2,000 hectares of scenic mountains, expanses of bogs and heaths, and grasslands. Some of the park's mountains, namely Benbaun, Bencullagh, Benbrack and Muckanaght, are part of the famous Twelve Bens range. Diamond Hill towers over the park visitor-centre.

Much of the present park-lands formed part of

the Kylemore Abbey estate and the Letterfrack Industrial School, the remainder having been purchased from private individuals.

Nature
Western blanket bog and heathland are the predominant vegetation types. Heathers clothe many of the mountain-sides, with three common species as well as the more unusual St Dabeoc's heath. Purple moor-grass grows in clumps in the bogs and is responsible for the colour of much of the landscape throughout the year. Sundews and butterworts trap insects with their leaves to gain nutrients, which are in short supply. Other common plants are lousewort, bog cotton, milkwort, bog asphodel, orchids and bog myrtle, with a variety of lichens and mosses.

Birdlife in the park is varied: meadow pipits, skylarks, stonechats, chaffinches, robins and wrens are just some of the common songbirds to be found there. Birds of prey are sometimes seen, usually kestrel, with sparrowhawk, merlin and peregrine falcon making occasional visits.

Native red deer once roamed the hills of Connemara but due to human pressures they became extinct some 150 years ago. Red deer are being reintroduced and already the nucleus of a herd has been established within the park. A herd of pure-bred Connemara Ponies has been established to assist in conserving this unique equine breed. Some of the present herd may be seen behind the visitor-centre.

Historic Heritage
Many remains of human presence can be seen in

St Dabeoc's Heath Connemara

View in Connemara
National Park

the park. The oldest is a megalithic court-tomb, some 4,000 years old. Close by is an early 19th-century graveyard. Also of that period is Tobar Mweelin, a well tapped to supply water to Kylemore Castle around 1870, which is still in use today. Stretches of the old Galway road, used over a century ago, may still be seen in the northern sections of the park. Ruined houses, a disused lime kiln, old sheep-pens, drainage systems and old walls in various parts of the park, are all evidence of a once-greater population in that area.

In the past the lands were used for agriculture, mainly as grazing for cattle and sheep. Vegetables were grown on some of the more fertile lowlands. Today, these areas are easily recognised by old cultivation ridges and hollows.

Open daily end May to end September 10.00-18.00 hours.

Enquiries phone (095) 41054.

Literature available at site.

Hill-walking, Connemara National Park

Connemara Ponies

Visitor Centre, Connemara National Park

Wildlife

GALWAY

Ballynastaig Wood
M42 03

This reserve, like Coole–Garryland below, is situated 3 km north-west of Gort, Co. Galway. Both reserves, through their combination of deciduous woods, limestone reefs, lakes and turloughs, constitute one of the most interesting Irish vegetation and faunal complexes still in existence.

GALWAY

Coole–Garryland
M42 03

Coole–Garryland reserve contains a variety of floral habitat, including well-formed high forest on

Lady's smock

deep pockets of soil, dwarf woodland on limestone pavement, bare pavement, a turlough complex in the hollows and Coole Lake.

A large portion of this reserve was formerly owned by Lady Gregory, co-founder with W. B. Yeats and Edward Martyn, of the Abbey Theatre in Dublin.

This site and Ballynastaig Wood above are open during daylight hours and there is an internal road network, along with a nature trail.

GALWAY

Derryclare
L84 50

The reserve is situated on the north-west shore of Derryclare Lough, Ballinahinch, Co. Galway. It is an excellent example of native semi-natural woodland of the hyper-oceanic type, of which about 8 hectares are woodland, the balance comprising pond, wet moorland and lake-shore ecosystems.

There is no direct public access, but it may be viewed across Derryclare Lake from the roadway.

GALWAY

Derrycrag Wood
M75 00

This reserve is 1.25 km south-east of Woodford and has all the features of Rosturra Wood opposite.

Both reserves are accessible at all times and there are internal road systems.

Coole-Garryland
Co. Galway

GALWAY

Pollnaknockaun Wood
M75 00

This wood is 1.5 km north-east of Woodford Village in Co. Galway. It is semi-natural woodland — oak/ash — which once formed part of the extensive forest referred to in the description of Rosturra and Derrycrag Woods.

It is accessible at all times and has an internal road system.

GALWAY

Richmond Esker
M59 54

This ridge is 4 km north-west of Moylough, Co. Galway. It is one of the few esker ridges left in

Ireland which still carries native woodland. Although now extensively planted with conifers and exotic species, the native woodland will be expanded by appropriate management techniques.

It is accessible at all times, but there are no visitor services.

GALWAY

Rosturra Wood
M75 00

This wood is situated 3 km north-east of Woodford in Co. Galway. It is a reserve that comprises fragments of a once extensive forest — as does Derrycrag Wood opposite. Both reserves now contain stands of oak and ash with an understorey of holly and hazel. They have a rich ground flora.

MAYO

Knockmoyle Sheskin
F98 25

The reserve is situated 8 km north of the Electricity Supply Board's power station at Bellacorrick in Co. Mayo, between the Oweniny River on the eastern side and Sheskin Lodge with Sheskin's mined settlement on the western side.

To be found here is an extensive cover of lowland blanket bog which is unsurpassed for its density and abundance of pools, streams and flushes. There are also patches of willow and birch scrub. It is one of the least disturbed blanket bog areas remaining in Ireland.

Access is not only very difficult, but it is also very dangerous.

MAYO

Oldhead Wood
L38 20

Oldhead Wood is 3 km north-east of Louisburgh in Co. Mayo. This small reserve lies on the east side of two knolls which form a promontory on the southern shore of Clew Bay. It is an example of semi-natural woodland, oak being the dominant species, with birch, rowan, willow and some introduced beech and sycamore.

It is accessible at all times with pathways and a picnic area.

MAYO

Owenboy
G05 16

Owenboy reserve is 10 km west of Crossmolina, and 10 km east of Bellacorrick on the southside of the Ballina/Belmullet road at Eskeragh Bridge. It is an area with features characteristic of both raised and blanket bogs. There are several very wet Sphagnum-dominated areas, flushes with poor fen and interesting mosses, as well as dry heathy ridges. Greenland whitefronted geese frequent it.

Parts of the bog are hazardous to cross and there are no visitor services.

*Knockmoyle/Sheskin
Co. Mayo*

Bog Bean

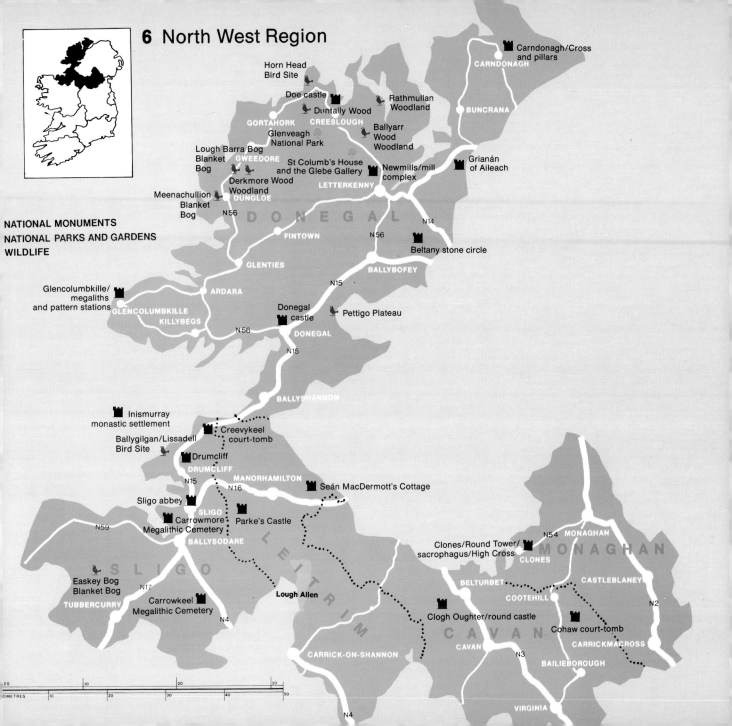

6 North West Region

NATIONAL MONUMENTS
NATIONAL PARKS AND GARDENS
WILDLIFE

Carndonagh/Cross and pillars

CARNDONAGH

Horn Head Bird Site

Doe castle

BUNCRANA

Rathmullan Woodland

Duntally Wood

GORTAHORK

CREESLOUGH

Ballyarr Wood Woodland

Glenveagh National Park

Lough Barra Bog Blanket Bog

GWEEDORE

St Columb's House and the Glebe Gallery

Newmills/mill complex

Grianán of Aileach

Derkmore Wood Woodland

LETTERKENNY

Meenachullion Blanket Bog

DUNGLOE

N56

DONEGAL

N14

FINTOWN

N56

Beltany stone circle

GLENTIES

BALLYBOFEY

Glencolumbkille/ megaliths and pattern stations

ARDARA

N15

GLENCOLUMBKILLE

KILLYBEGS

Donegal castle

Pettigo Plateau

N56

DONEGAL

N15

BALLYSHANNON

Inismurray monastic settlement

Creevykeel court-tomb

Ballygilgan/Lissadell Bird Site

Drumcliff

DRUMCLIFF

N15

MANORHAMILTON

Seán MacDermott's Cottage

N16

Sligo abbey

SLIGO

LEITRIM

Parke's Castle

Carrowmore Megalithic Cemetery

BALLYSODARE

N59

Clones/Round Tower/ sacrophagus/High Cross

MONAGHAN

N54

CLONES

MONAGHAN

SLIGO

Easkey Bog Blanket Bog

N17

Lough Allen

BELTURBET

CASTLEBLANEY

Carrowkeel Megalithic Cemetery

COOTEHILL

N2

TUBBERCURRY

N4

Clogh Oughter/round castle

Cohaw court-tomb

CAVAN

CARRICKMACROSS

CARRICK-ON-SHANNON

CAVAN

N3

BAILIEBOROUGH

N4

VIRGINIA

MILES
10   20   30
KILOMETRES
10   20   30   40   50

National Monuments

DONEGAL

Beltany/stone circle
C25 00

The very suitably-named Tops Hill, 3.2 km (two miles) south of Raphoe, is crowned by one of the largest stone circles in the country. A total of sixty stones make up a circle 44.20 m in diameter, and outside it is a single upright stone. In more easterly parts of the country, local puritanical folklore saw in such solitary stones a musician, and in the circle of stones a ring of dancers, all of whom had been turned into stone because they had committed the sin of making merry on the sabbath.

But the local name of this Donegal ring, Beltany, while not apparently being recorded in traditional folklore, could suggest that the site may somehow have seen associated with the pagan Celtic May Day festival, at which the advent of summer was celebrated, in the hope of averting dangers which might threaten cattle and the dairy. Judging by stone circles in other parts of the country, however, the Beltany circle may well go back to remoter, pre-Celtic times — perhaps as early as *c.* 2000 BC.

DONEGAL

Carndonagh/High Cross and pillars
C47 45

A holy well at Carndonagh was dedicated to St Patrick, suggesting that the place may have had some connection with the national apostle, who may possibly have created a bishopric here.

But the interesting group of early stone monuments at Carndonagh date from centuries after St Patrick's time. Three of these are grouped together on a roadside platform outside the Church of Ireland grounds. The tallest of them is a ringless cross decorated on one face with interlace ornament, and on the other, with an interlaced cross beneath which is a simple crucifixion scene. The three figures below may represent the Holy Women coming to the Tomb. The cross has

Doe Castle

frequently been dated to the 7th century and seen to be among the earliest High Crosses. But recent research suggests that the cross may be as late as the 9th or 10th century, and a product of a local school of stonemasons having connections with Scotland.

Beside it are two pillars, one carved with a harpist — David — and a warrior — Goliath — and the other with, *inter alia*, a figure with curious ears. In the churchyard grounds* is another remarkable pillar with a further representation of the crucified Christ, and a *flabellum* or liturgical fan, possibly a relic of St Columba, the famous Donegal saint. Beside the church doorway is a decorated church lintel, probably of 12th-century date.

*Not in the care of the Office of Public Works.

DONEGAL

Doe Castle
C08 32

Situated on a piece of land jutting out into an Atlantic inlet near Creeslough, is Doe Castle which gets its name from the family which built it in the 16th-century — Mac Sweeney na dTuath [Mac Sweeney na Doe], and one of the family tombstones of the time is still preserved in the castle. The impressive central tower of the castle is surrounded by a powerful bawn-wall, protected on three sides by the sea, and on a fourth by a ditch cut into the rock. It was in these stony, yet romantic surroundings, that the famous Red Hugh O'Donnell was fostered.

As one of Donegal's strongest fortifications, Doe experienced to the full the see-saw history of the north-west of Ireland during the 17th century. Sir Cahir O'Doherty set up his headquarters here before this attack on Derry in 1608; assigned to a Planter only a few years later, the castle was recovered by the Mac Sweeneys in 1641; Owen Roe O'Neill landed here in his effort to undo the effects of the Ulster Plantation. After the Restoration of Charles II, it served as an Emnglish military outpost, and was finally

Carndonagh Cross and Pillars

repossessed by the Mac Sweeneys during the Williamite wars. Restored around 1800, it was occupied until around the beginning of this century.

DONEGAL

Donegal/castle
G93 78

Dún na nGall — 'the fort of the foreigners' — refers to a settlement of the Vikings, but the town owes its present form to other settlers — the Planters brought from Britain by Sir Basil Brooke in the first decade of the 17th century.

Not far from the Diamond, the town's main focus, is the castrle which Sir Basil made his home in 1610. A fine rectangular tower existed already on the site, built by the O'Donnells about a century earlier, and this tower Sir Basil proceeded to appropriate unto himself after the Flight of the Earls in 1607. He transformed it from a fortress into a comfortable residence by adding

Donegal Castle

gables and windows, and making the first floor into a banqueting hall, presided over by a sculpturally-interesting fireplace bearing fruit and his own coat of arms.

At right angles to this tower Sir Basil added an attractive gabled Jacobean manor-house, with a decorative entrance doorway on the south side. Sir Basil strengthened O'Donnell's original bawn-wall surrounding the castle by the addition, among other things, of a strong gate tower.

The whole gives some idea of the style which the Planter élite introduced after they had replaced the old Gaelic aristocracy.

Open daily mid-June to September 10.00-18.00 hours.
Enquiries phone (073) 22405.
Literature available at site.

DONEGAL

Glencolumbkille/megaliths and pattern stations
G52-54 82-85

St Columba, or Colmcille, was one of the most human, yet also one of the most dynamic saints to have emerged in early Ireland. Fiery and occasionally impulsive in temperament, diplomatic by nature, and a contrite sinner at heart, he saved the bards — and poetry — in Ireland from the danger of extinction. He was born in Gartan, near Glenveagh Castle in Co. Donegal in the year 521, and founded monasteries at Derry and Durrow before voluntarily exiling himself to the Hebridean island of Iona, from whence he evangelised the Picts, and where he died in 597.

Other than Derry [Doire Cholmcille], one place which still bears his name is the beautifully-secluded Glencolumbkille in south-west Donegal, where the saint is still venerated annually by a *turas* [pattern], or day-pilgrimage, on his feast-day of 9 June. The pilgrims visit fifteen 'stations' throughout the valley, many of which are marked by a collection of Early Christian decorated stones.

South-west of the valley is Malin, with its varied

Grianán of Aileach

selection of megalithic tombs. Their builders, and those who later came to pay homage to St Columba, are more likely to have come by sea rather than by land, as the area was more easily accessible by water than by land in the days before the hard-surfaced road was built over the hills which form, not only a scenic backdrop to the valley, but also a barrier separating it from its hinterland.

DONEGAL

Grianán of Aileach/stone fort
C37 20

Few monuments provide the visitor with a more exhilarating panorama than the stone fort, known as the Grianán of Aileach, perched on a hill-top at the centre of a triangle encompassing Derry, Buncrana and Letterkenny, and looking out over the Foyle and Swilly estuaries. The word Grianán means a sunny place or a palace, and Aileach was the ancient capital of the north-western branch of

Newmills, Mill Complex

Carrowkeel, passage-tomb cemetery

the Uí Néill, the great ruling dynasty of the first five hundred years of Christian Ireland. But it still remains a mystery as to whether this great round stone fort was built during or before the Early Christian period. Its location, and the interior stairways giving defenders quick access to the parapets, certainly suggest that it was built for protection, probably by a local chieftain whose long-vanished dwelling lay within the wall.

Outside the fort the keen eye will be able to detect the slight traces of a total of three earthen rings, which acted as outer defences. The stone fort was demolished in 1101 by Murtagh O'Brien, King of Munster, who ordered each of his soldiers to take a stone from the fort away with him on his way back to Limerick.

The present shape of the fort owes much to the restoration by Dr Bernard, Bishop of Derry, in 1879, and a further ecclesiastical connection is the inspiration which it gave in 1967 to the round church at Burt, which stands in its shadow at the bottom of the hill.

DONEGAL

Newmills/mill complex
C12 08

The first venture of the Office of Public Works into the realm of industrial archaeology in the northern half of the country was the recent acquisition of a mill complex at Newmills, about 4.5 km (three miles) west of Letterkenny.

The oldest surviving building is said to be 300 or 400 years old, and it was only in 1982 that the Gallagher family finally brought to a close the milling business which had been conducted there for centuries. Water for the mill-wheels is siphoned off from the river Swilly at a place known as 'The Carry' almost a quarter of a mile upstream from the mill. There, a special salmon weir has now been constructed, and new sluice gates completed to control the amount of water getting to the mill-wheels along the partially-piped mill-race.

There are two mills. The upper one was for flax, used in the making of linen, and much of the old machinery is still in place; the water which turned the wheel for the flax-mill then flowed further to turn what is one of the largest surviving mill-wheels in Ireland — that made by the Stevenson foundry in Strabane in 1867 — for the grinding of barley and oats in the lower mill. The whole complex is an interesting reminder of a stage in the industrial development of this country which has now given way to a more sophisticated, but visually far less fascinating, technology.

SLIGO

Carrowkeel/passage-tomb cemetery
G76 11

Carrowkeel is a 'classic' passage-tomb cemetery, located on an eerie series of flat-topped ridges with a truly breathtaking view over Lough Arrow and beyond. Partially overlain by a covering of turf, since they were built some 5,000 years ago, many of the tombs have preserved their original features in a remarkably intact state, though access to the interior is often perilous, not to say dangerous, at times. Well-meaning archaeologists managed to 'excavate' the mounds after a fashion during the course of a mere few weeks in 1911, and showed that some of the mounds contained no obvious tombs, while others contained box-like cists. But the best have tombs with a cross-shaped plan, that is with a passage leading into a central chamber with one or two side chambers leading off it on each side, and with one at the back.

One of the tombs, known as Cairn E, had a passage-tomb at one end and a court-tomb at the other, thus combining the two major tomb types of Stone Age Ireland, and suggesting a contemporaneity in building styles. Unlike the passage-tombs of Co. Meath (see page 144), those at Carrowkeel lack the geometrical patterns ornamenting the stones of the tombs. A neighbouring ridge has a series of round huts, but it has never been possible to prove that these actually housed the tomb-builders during the course of construction.

SLIGO

Carrowmore/megalithic cemetery
G66 33

The area of Carrowmore, about 4.5 km (three miles) west of Sligo town, once contained what was, arguably, the largest assemblage of megalithic tombs in the whole of Europe. Though spread over many square kilometres, they had the misfortune to have been built upon a gravel ridge, which proved such an attraction to the local quarrymen during the last hundred years, that it is now but a skeleton of its former self.

Despite despoliation, a remarkable group of monuments survives and will be preserved. Being well spaced out in the landscape, the individual monuments take some finding, but the diligent searcher will be rewarded with dolmens and stone circles, or both combined. Some were excavated around 1980 by a Swedish interdisciplinary team, and are likely to be at least as early as, if not earlier than, the great tombs of the Boyne valley (see page 144).

One of the best prehistoric perspectives in Ireland is provided by the view over one of these dolmens to 'Queen Maeve's Grave' on top of Knocknarea, which itself is the largest unopened megalithic tomb in the country.

Open daily mid-June to Sepember 10.00-18.00 hours.

Literature available at site.

SLIGO

Creevykeel/court-tomb
G72 54

Creevykeel, close to the Sligo-Bundoran road, is one of the most extensive court-tombs in the country. This type of tomb is found distributed over a large swathe of territory, stretching across Ulster and as far as Mayo, and together with the passage-tombs which are generally found further to the south, they make up the major portion of the megalithic tombs of Stone Age Ireland.

Built probably in the 4th and 3rd millennium BC, these tombs can have a variety of forms, based on an open forecourt giving access to a galleried and stone-covered burial chamber. Creevykeel is one of the more 'baroque' variants, having an open oval-shaped court delimited by upright stones, with an entrance in the east, and giving access to the tomb-gallery at the opposite end of the court. Behind this tomb are the remnants of two others, possibly later additions.

Unlike the passage-tombs, which are frequently clustered into cemeteries located on high ground, the court-tombs are more scattered and, like Creevykeel, they have a preference for the lower and better-drained soils. In addition, they

Passage-tomb at Carrowmore

may have played a role in local magical ritual, perhaps as a focal meeting point for the powerful families of the locality who could legitimise their right to hold the land by preserving the remains of their ancestors who had originally taken possession of the territory.

SLIGO

Drumcliff/High Cross and Round Tower
G68 42

Conveniently located beside the Sligo-Bundoran road, Drumcliff combines the grave of W. B. Yeats,* which is in the Church of Ireland graveyard,* and the remains of a monastery possibly founded by St Columba, and therefore belonging to the group of monasteries known as the *paruchia Columbae* associated with him and which also includes Iona and Kells.

Other than the stump of a Round Tower located on the southern side of the road, the most important survivor of the monastery is the High Cross, variously dated between the 9th and the 11th centuries, which stands beside the cul-de-sac leading down to the Church of Ireland church.

The cross consists of two parts which are roughly contemporary, but may not have belonged together. The east face bears scenes of *Adam and Eve, David slaying Goliath, Daniel in the Lions' Den*, and *Christ as Judge*, but — other than *The Crucifixion* — the scenes on the west face present considerable problems of interpretation. The end of the south arm of the cross bears the only surviving High Cross representation of the *Virgin and Child*, reminiscent of the more famous example adorning a page of that great Columban codex — the *Book of Kells*.

*Not in the care of the Office of Public Works.

SLIGO

Inismurray/early monastic settlement
G57 54

Inismurray, a remarkable and quite extensive

Creevykeel, court-tomb

Drumcliff High Cross

119

island lying some 5.4 km (four miles) off the coast of Co. Sligo, is said to derive its name from St Muiredaig, the first bishop of Killala at the time of St Patrick. But the monastery on the island was founded not by him but by a St Laisren, or Molaise, one of the many saints bearing the latter name who lived in the 6th century.

The focus of this monastery is a D-shaped enclosure surrounded by a high wall, which some think may have existed before the foundation of the monastery. Within this enclosure, which is divided into three parts, is a collection of churches and beehive huts, as well as cross-decorated slabs and the famous cursing stones used to bring down a malediction on one's enemies.

Dotted throughout the island are numerous *leachtaí* [memorials] and prayer-stations, at which many pilgrims over the centuries have prayed. The island, on which it is often difficult to land, depending on wind and tidal conditions, represents one of the most remarkable clusters of Early Christian monuments anywhere in the country.

*Monastic Cashel,
Inismurray*

Sligo Friary

SLIGO

Sligo/abbey
G69 36

Like many a Norman town in Ireland, Sligo had its castle and its 'abbey'. The former has now disappeared, but the 'abbey' is still preserved. It was in reality, a Dominican friary founded by Maurice Fitzgerald around 1253, and the choir, with its fine row of tall, thin lancet windows, was built not long after the foundation.

The altar, one of the few medieval examples surviving in the country, is probably 15th century in date, at which time the present east window was inserted. One unusual feature is the partially-reconstructed 15th-century rood screen which separated the church from the nave, and which was probably surmounted by a carved crucifixion ('rood') originally.

The church contains two interesting grave monuments worthy of note, the medieval O'Crean

tomb of 1506 opposite the present entrance, with its *Crucifixion* and flanking saints as 'weepers', and the Renaissance-style O'Conor Sligo monument of 1624, located high up in the south-eastern corner of the chancel.

The sacristy and chapter house date from the 13th-century, but the cloister and the remaining conventual buildings were added two centuries later.

LEITRIM

Laghty Barr/Seán MacDermott's Cottage
G99 42

Seán Mac Diarmada, otherwise Seán MacDermott, was one of signatories of the Proclamation of the Irish Republic, proclaimed at the General Post Office in Dublin in April of 1916. For this, in the following month, he paid the ultimate penalty at the hands of a British firing-squad. Before his death, he wrote a touching

Parke's Castle

Boyle Abbey

and truly noble letter to his family, a copy of which is preserved in the cottage where he was born and reared in the rugged and beautiful, landscape of that part of Co. Leitrim overlooking Lough Macnean.

The thatched farmhouse, which was his birthplace, and the outbuildings, are presented as they would have appeared in his youth. The vernacular buildings and the beds, chairs, dressers and cooking utensils bear witness to the simple life-style of a self-supporting people.

LEITRIM

Parke's Castle
G78 35

Parke's Castle, on the Leitrim side of the border with Co. Sligo on the northern shores of Lough Gill, now provides the visitor with one of the most unexpected and interesting attractions in the whole north-west of the country, thanks to the ingenious work of restoration carried out during the 1980s.

This was preceded by an excavation which unearthed the foundation of a 16th-century O'Rourke tower in the centre of the courtyard of the castle which the Planter Robert Parke built beside it in the 1620s.

Parke's original fortification consisted merely of a small tower which is now the entrance to the complex, but after he had regained the possessions, which he lost during the Cromwellian wars, he built on the rooms adjoining it to the north. The whole has now been fittingly restored with native Irish oak flooring, roofing and panelling of the highest quality, to provide exhibitions, together with an audio-visual introduction to the Castle and the national monuments of the region.

The courtyard next to the east wing, surrounded by Parke's stout bawn-wall, has also been provided with restored buildings, including an example of

a working forge and a tea room where visitors can refresh themselves.

Open daily mid-June to mid-September 9.00-18.30 hours.
Enquiries phone (071) 64149.
Literature available at site.

CAVAN

Clogh Oughter/round castle
H35 04

Clogh Oughter castle takes up a goodly portion of the small, rocky island on which it stands in the waters of Lough Oughter. But, as the level of the lake was originally higher than it is today, the castle may once have occupied virtually the whole island, and it was described in the 17th century as rising directly out of the lake. It is one of a small number of circular 13th century keeps.

The four storeys of this massive tower reach a height of about 16.77 m, and it has an internal diameter of about 10.67 m. The castle may have been built in the de Lacy family in the early 13th century and soon after captured by the O'Reilly's. The O'Rourke's captured it from them in 1327 only to return it to the O'Reilly's for a mere twenty cows.

The castle was ideally suited to serve as a prison, which it often did, and one of its more famous inmates (in 1641-42) was William Bedell, the Bishop of Kilmore and translator of the first printed Irish version of the Old Testament.

CAVAN

Cohaw/court-tomb
H64 13

Right across Ulster and as far west as Mayo, Stone Age men built impressive stone tombs in which to bury their dead. These are known today as court-tombs, or court-cairns, because one of their characteristic features is a semi-circular court, sometimes paved with flag-stones. It was from this court that entrance would have been gained to the actual tomb-chamber, which was frequently subdivided into a number of interlinked sections, often roofed by heavy capstones.

The basic form of a court and adjoining burial chamber was varied in a number of ways. Cohaw shows one of these variants, in which two such court-and-tomb units are placed back to back with no access from one to the other. As court-tombs are usually miles apart, we may take it that they represent the central burial focus for a community spread over many square miles, and who — by holding the remains of their forebears — were giving monumental expression to their claim to the lands of their ancestors. However, the only human remains which came to light during an excavation in 1949 were the cremated bones of a child and a youth's skull. The pottery, which was also unearthed, shows the tomb to have been built, probably, sometime around 3000 BC.

MONAGHAN

Clones/Round Tower/sarcophagus/High Cross
H50 26

Co. Monaghan's largest collection of monuments is in the town of Clones, where the local saint, Tighernach, founded a monastery sometime before his death in 550. It was doubtless located in the graveyard in which the Round Tower stands.

Nearby, is a unique stone in the shape of a sarcophagus, with a carved figure as well as decorated finials and hinges, which doubtless imitate in stone the wooden and metal reliquary containing the bones of the founding saint. Though it is difficult to ascertain the date of the original reliquary on which it was modelled, the stone sarcophagus was almost certainly carved in the 12th century.

Dating from a few centuries earlier is the High Cross, now standing in the Diamond at the centre of the town. It consists of the shaft of one cross and the head of another, mounted together, though the top portion is only a few centuries old. The shaft has scenes from the Old Testament, including *Adam and Eve,* on one face, and on the other, representations of events from the New Testament, such as the *Adoration of the Magi,* the *Marriage Feast of Cana* and the *Miracle of the Loaves and Fishes.* The head of the cross has *Daniel in the Lions' Den* on one face, and a *Crucifixion* on the other.

Clones High Cross

National Parks and Gardens

DONEGAL

Glenveagh National Park
C02

Glenveagh National Park lies along the Derryveagh Mountains in the north-west of Co. Donegal. This 9,667 hectares of mountain, moorland, lakes and woods is cut in two by the spectacular valley which gives the park its name — Glenveagh.

In 1975, the lands of Glenveagh were purchased from Mr Henry McIlhenny of Philadelphia, USA, by the Office of Public Works. In 1981 Mr McIlhenny presented Glenveagh Castle and gardens to the Irish nation, thereby adding greatly to the amenities of the National Park.

The magic of Glenveagh derives from its being one of the last places in Ireland to be influenced by man.

Nature

The park lands include the peaks of the two highest mountains in Donegal, Errigal and Slieve Snaght, and there are many other fine hills, notably Dooish and Leahanmore.

At the south-west end of the park are the ice-carved cliffs of the Poisoned Glen and Bingorm, while the north-east end has a gentler array of hills, deep peat bogs and the swampy valley of the Owencarrow river.

There are lakes ranging in size from little hillside lochans, or lakelets, to the majestic Lough Veagh, which is surrounded by the scattered remains of a forest which once covered much of Donegal. The ancient name of Derryveagh means

'forest of oak and birch' and, today, these trees remain the important species in the woods.

Glenveagh is home to the largest herd of red deer in Ireland. A twenty-eight mile fence — believed by some to be the longest fence in the country — was erected in the 1890s to contain the deer herd, and it is maintained still. The deer spend most of the summer on high ground, returning to more sheltered areas during winter or summer storms.

In summer the hillsides are dotted with two yellow flowers — tormentil and bog asphodel. The most frequently encountered birds on the uplands are the meadow pipit, stonechats, grouse, ravens; peregrines and merlins are to be seen occasionally.

The woodlands of Glenveagh support a luxuriant growth of mosses and filmy fern and a large area has been fenced off from the deer to allow young trees to survive so that the forest may regenerate. The woods are inhabited by badgers, foxes and stoats, and woodland bird-life includes siskins, tree-creepers, redstarts and wood warblers.

Lough Veagh has natural stocks of brown trout, sea trout and salmon.

Glenveagh Castle and Its History

Few buildings in Ireland can boast as fine a setting as Glenveagh Castle, a castellated mansion standing atop a slight promontory that juts into Lough Veagh. Built from rough-hewn granite, it consists of a four-storey rectangular keep with walls 1.5 metres thick, along with battlemented ramparts and a Round Tower.

The estate of Glenveagh was created by John

Glenveagh Castle and Lough Veagh

George Adair in 1857-9, by purchasing several smaller holdings. He attained an infamous reputation throughout Donegal — and the whole of Ireland — by evicting all of his 254 tenants on the Glenveagh estate in the cold April of 1861.

Adair built Glenveagh Castle about 1870, but died in 1885. His wife survived him until 1921 and, unlike her husband, she is remembered as a kind and generous person. The castle was occupied by the IRA in 1922, but they evacuated it when the Free State Army arrived. The latter used the building as a garrison for three years, before leaving the glen to its normal tranquil ways.

From 1937 to 1983 Glenveagh was the summer residence of Henry McIlhenny, a wealthy Philadelphian art collector of Donegal ancestry. His furnishings remain in many of the rooms.

Glenveagh Gardens

The luxuriance of the gardens around Glenveagh Castle contrasts starkly with the austere mountains on all sides. First conceived more than a hundred years ago, the gardens boast a multitude of exotic plants whose survival here attests to the careful nurturing they have received over many years.

Work on the gardens began under the direction

The Walled Garden Glenveagh

Glenveagh Castle

of Mrs Adair and the subsequent efforts of Henry McIlhenny have resulted in gardens of extraordinary charm. Pines and rhododendrons provide a windbreak against frequent gales to allow delicate plants, from as far afield as Chile, Madeira and Tasmania, to survive and flourish. Sculptures, formal features and vistas to the lake add elements of surprise among the naturalistic plantings.

Open daily Easter to end of October 10.30-18.30 hours.
Open Sundays June to August 10.30-19.30 hours.
Closed Mondays in April and October except bank holiday Mondays.
Enquiries phone (074) 37090.

DONEGAL

St Columb's House and the Glebe Gallery
C06 17

St Columb's House and the Glebe Gallery, just a short distance from Glenveagh National Park and managed in conjunction with it, is the home of the Derek Hill collection.

Originally built as a rectory — later to become a small fishing hotel — the house was for thirty years the home of Derek Hill who transformed it into a place of beauty and curiosity.

Mr Hill is an artist of international repute, noted particularly not only for his portraits and his Tory Island paintings, but also as a great collector. His collections include paintings by leading Irish, British and Italian artists, pottery, glass and ceramics, oriental prints, embroidered cloths and rugs, beautiful furniture with curtains and wallpaper designed by William Morris.

In 1980, Derek Hill presented his house, grounds and collections to the State, and the Glebe Gallery was then constructed in the courtyard beside the house.

Today the Hill collection can be viewed in that gallery and in the house itself, where visitors can enjoy a treasure trove of artefacts of all varieties presented in an informal atmosphere far removed from a conventional museum. The house and gallery are set in attractive grounds by the shores of Lough Gartan.

Open daily Easter Week 11.00-18.30 hours.
Tuesday to Saturday end May to end September 11.00-18.30 hours.
Sundays 13.00-18.00 hours.
Closed Monday.
Enquiries phone (074) 37071.

Head of Lough Veagh

Red stags, Glenveagh

*St Columb's House
and grounds*

Glebe Gallery

Drawing-room in St Columb's House

Wildlife

DONEGAL

Ballyarr Wood
C18 20

The wood is situated 11 km north of Letterkenny and 5 km west of Rathmelton on the eastern flank of a low ridge of hills. There is an oak-wood growing on a range of soil types and there is a rich flora there. It contains areas of old coppice and old field systems reverting to woodland.

It is accessible at all times but there are no visitor services.

DONEGAL

Derkmore Wood
G78 99

This reserve is situated in Gweebarra Forest, Co. Donegal, on exposed undulating ground on the southern flank of Cleangort Hill. It is an area of oak scrub with well-developed bryophyte and lichen flora.

It is accessible at all times but there are no visitor services.

DONEGAL

Duntally Wood
C06 39

This is a wood situated in a deep valley 500 m south-east of Creeslough in Co. Donegal. It is rich in plant species with alder woodland on the valley floor and hazel/ash woodland on the valley sides.

It is accessible at all times but it has no visitor services.

DONEGAL

Horn Head
C00 42

This refuge for fauna covers 9 km of the north-facing cliffs at Horn Head. The cliffs, composed of quartzite, are vertical — or nearly vertical — along most of their expanse, which make safe nesting sites for a variety of seabirds, notably kittiwakes, guillemots, razorbills and puffins. Other breeding birds include fulmars, herring gulls, cormorants, shags, common gulls, black guillemots, raven, chough, peregrines, rock pipits and twites.

The cliffs themselves are inaccessible to all but experienced climbers. There are ruined buildings, such as the Coast Guard Station and signal tower, near the cliffs' edge, which have pathways leading to them.

Bee orchid

Bog asphodel

Horn Head, Co. Donegal

Small groups of people may approach the cliff top in these regions, but great care should be exercised as the cliffs are dangerous.

DONEGAL

Lough Barra Bog
B92 11

The bog is situated just south of Glenveagh National Park — see National Parks and Gardens, p. 126 — north-east of the Glenties town. It is part of an extensive and characteristic area of lowland blanket bog with numerous pools and small lakes.

The Gweebarra River flows through the bog which is a habitat for merlins, golden plover and Greenland white-fronted geese.

It is accessible at all times via the Lettermacward–Churchill road immediately west

Snipe

Curlew

Lough Barra Bog, Co. Donegal

of Lough Barra. There are no visitor services and there is a need for caution as parts of this bog are very soft and can be unsafe.

DONEGAL

Meenachullion
B92 07

The reserve is situated on the southern edge of the Lough Barra blanket bog complex north of Gubben Hill. It is an area of lowland blanket bog vegetation, grading into wet grassy heath on the slopes of the hill, with small, but eroded, areas of highland blanket bog on the flat top of Gubben Hill.

There is no direct public access.

DONEGAL

Pettigo Plateau
H02 74

The plateau is 10 km south-east of Donegal town and the reserve is an area with numerous rock outcrops, lakes and streams with a mixture of blanket bog and wet heath. It is a wintering site for Greenland white-fronted geese. Forests surround the reserve on the eastern and southern sides.

There is no direct public access.

DONEGAL

Rathmullan Wood
C27 27

Situated on the eastern shore of Lough Swilly 20 km north-east of Letterkenny is where this reserve is to be found. Its oak wood has a well-developed structure and it is rich in plant species.

It is accessible at all times but there are no visitor services.

SLIGO

Ballygilgan, Lissadell
G64 44

This reserve is situated between the public road

Bog violet

135

from Carney to Lissadell in Co. Sligo and the seashore. It is a large field and, since the turn of the century, it has been an internationally important wintering ground for barnacle geese.

These geese arrive in October and remain there until April. The flock using the area is the largest in the Irish mainland and constitutes 17 per cent of the Irish wintering population. Its international importance lies in its holding of over 8 per cent of the total Greenland breeding population.

The geese are easily viewed from a hide which is located at the western end of the reserve.

SLIGO

Easkey Bog
G47 27

This bog is situated on the northern side of the Ox Mountains. It is one of the few extensive areas of highland blanket bog in the country. It is intermediate between lowland and mountain blanket bog and the area grades into mountain blanket bog to the south, while an extensive area of lowland blanket bog occurs about 2 km to the west.

There is no general access to this site and the bog is unsafe.

Sea bindweed

Bog oak

Bog cotton

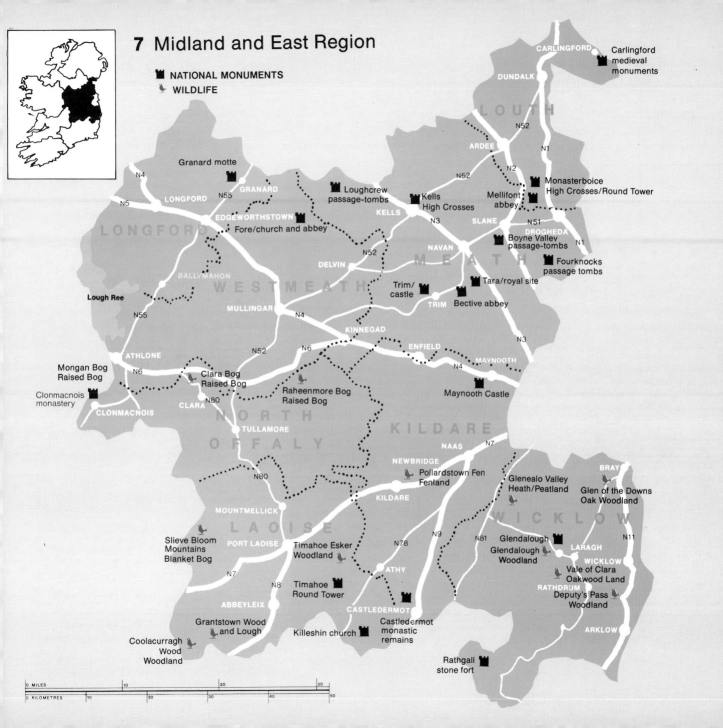

7 Midland and East Region

🏰 NATIONAL MONUMENTS
🦆 WILDLIFE

Carlingford medieval monuments

CARLINGFORD

DUNDALK

LOUTH

N1

N52

ARDEE

N52

N2

Monasterboice High Crosses/Round Tower

Mellifont abbey

SLANE

DROGHEDA

N51

N1

Granard motte

GRANARD

LONGFORD

N4

N55

N5

EDGEWORTHSTOWN

Fore/church and abbey

Loughcrew passage-tombs

Kells High Crosses

KELLS

N3

NAVAN

MEATH

Boyne Valley passage-tombs

Fourknocks passage tombs

LONGFORD

BALLYMAHON

WESTMEATH

DELVIN

N52

Trim/castle

TRIM

Tara/royal site

Bective abbey

N3

Lough Ree

N55

MULLINGAR

N4

KINNEGAD

N6

ENFIELD

MAYNOOTH

N4

ATHLONE

N6

N52

Mongan Bog Raised Bog

Clara Bog Raised Bog

Raheenmore Bog Raised Bog

Maynooth Castle

Clonmacnois monastery

CLONMACNOIS

CLARA

N80

NORTH

OFFALY

TULLAMORE

KILDARE

NAAS

N7

NEWBRIDGE

Pollardstown Fen Fenland

Glenealo Valley Heath/Peatland

BRAY

Glen of the Downs Oak Woodland

N80

KILDARE

WICKLOW

N11

MOUNTMELLICK

LAOISE

Slieve Bloom Mountains Blanket Bog

PORT LAOISE

Timahoe Esker Woodland

N78

N9

N81

Glendalough

Glendalough Woodland

LARAGH

Vale of Clara Oakwood Land

WICKLOW

RATHDRUM

Deputy's Pass Woodland

N7

N8

Timahoe Round Tower

ABBEYLEIX

Grantstown Wood and Lough

Killeshin church

CASTLEDERMOT

ATHY

Castledermot monastic remains

Coolacurragh Wood Woodland

Rathgall stone fort

ARKLOW

0 MILES   10   20   30

0 KILOMETRES   10   20   30   40   50

National Monuments

LOUTH

Carlingford/medieval monuments
J19 12

The town of Carlingford, attractively situated on the sea lough which bears its name, owes its origins to the castle, allegedly founded by King John, who stayed here for a mere three days in 1210.

The castle, standing on an imposing rock

Carlingford Castle

outcrop overlooking the harbour, was entered from the west through the space between two gate towers, which was only wide enough to have allowed one horseman through at a time. The whole of the eastern part of the castle, including the tall crossing wall, was probably built around 1262. With protection like this, it is no wonder that a thriving town grew up at the castle's foot. Many interesting relics of it survive, including remains of the town wall, of which the tower of the Church of Ireland church once formed a part.

'The Mint', where money was allegedly made, was set up around 1467 in a building interestingly decorated with Celtic interlace and other ornaments.

Other notable buildings* in the town are the Thotsel, originally a town gate and later a municipal meeting house, which spanned the street, and a tower house known as Taafe's Castle.
*Not in the care of the Office of Public Works.

LOUTH

Mellifont/Cistercian abbey
O01 78

The Hildebrandine reforms which began to sweep across Europe in the later 11th century came to fruition in Ireland during the 12th century through the energetic activity of St Malachy, the Archbishop of Armagh. Arising from his friendship with St Bernard of Clairvaux, he succeeded in encouraging the Cistercian monks to make their first Irish foundation at Mellifont [*the fount of honey*] in the peaceful valley of the River Mattock.

The Reformation and subsequent spoliation

The Lavabo, Mellifont Abbey

have dealt unkindly with the architectural remains of the monastery, but the foundations of the first Romanesque church of 1142, and its later Gothic successor, can still be made out, together with the attractive remnants of the claustral buildings, including the unique octagonal lavabo of *c.* 1210. Mellifont, as it turned out, was to be the first of many Cistercian foundations in Ireland and, within decades, many of the old Irish monasteries became depopulated.

Those people who wanted to become monks flocked instead to the Cistercians, who introduced not only a new continental monastic order to the country, but also a new and much more imposing order of architecture, consisting of a church and living quarters around a quadrangular cloister — an idea which was to inspire much monastic building of the later Middle Ages in Ireland. Open daily mid-June to mid-September 10.00–18.00 hours.

Tuesday to Saturday May to mid-June 10.00–13.00
hours and 14.00–17.00 hours.
Sunday 14.00–17.00 hours.
Enquiries phone (041) 26459.
Literature available at site.

*Muiredach's
Cross
Monasterboice*

LOUTH

Monasterboice/High Crosses/Round Tower
O04 82

Monasterboice gets its name from a monastery
founded by a little-known saint named Buite, who
died in 521. Its main attractions today are two of
the most important old Irish High Crosses, usually
dated to the 10th century, but belonging more
probably to the 9th. Of these, the best preserved is
that known as the Cross of Muiredach, because of
an inscription on the bottom of the west face of the
shaft, asking for a prayer for an, as yet,
unsatisfactorily identified person named
Muiredach who had the cross made.

Like many others, the cross has a *Crucifixion* at
the centre of the west face, and a *Last Judgment*
on the east face — the latter, with its rich imagery
of good and bad souls, being one of the earliest
surviving representations of the scene, and also the
most populated single scene of any of the Irish
High Crosses. In addition, the cross bears many
scenes from the Old and New Testaments, and at
least one panel, illustrating the life of the desert
fathers — Paul and Anthony.

The other cross, known as the West, or Tall,
Cross, is — at over 6.4 m — the tallest surviving
High Cross. It stands close to the Round Tower,
which dominates the whole site. This cross is also
rich in biblical sculpture, including scenes
illustrating the *Passion and Death of Christ*. The
west face of the head of the cross, with a probable
representation of David, is particularly well-
preserved.

In a railed area in the north-eastern part of the
graveyard, there are further cross fragments, and
an early Irish sun-dial.

MEATH

Bective/Cistercian abbey
N86 60

The abbey was founded in 1150 by Murchadh
O Melaghlin, King of Meath, for the Cistercians,

Bective Abbey

and dedicated to the Blessed Virgin. It is one of the earliest Cistercian abbeys in Ireland. The Abbot sat in the Parliament of the Pale. Hugh de Lacy's body was buried here in 1195 but, after a dispute, it was later transferred to St Thomas's in Dublin.

Of the original 12th-century abbey, only remnants of the south of the nave arcade, parts of the south transept, the chapter house, part of the west wing of the domestic buildings and some of the doorways in the south wing, remain.

In the 15th century, the buildings were fortified and great changes took place. The southern arcade of the nave was blocked up, the present cloister and many of the buildings around it, excluding the chapter house, were built. This cloister is the best feature of the abbey; one of the pillars bears a figure carrying a crozier. The tower, and the great hall in the south wing — probably the monks' refectory — were also added in this period.

At some later period further alterations took

Winter Solstice, Newgrange

Newgrange Tumulus

*Main Chamber
Newgrange*

place in the south transept; the oven between the south transept and the chapter house was inserted, and an external entrance to the south range was also added. The monastery was suppressed in 1536. In the following year, the abbey and its lands were leased to Thomas Agarde, and they were bought by Andrew Wyse in 1552. Subsequently it passed to the Dillons and then to the Boltons.

MEATH

The Boyne Valley/passage-tombs
O00 72

The rich soils of the Boyne Valley have attracted farmers to settle there since Stone Age days of 5,000 years ago. The area has always been something of an historical melting-pot: it was there that 'King Billy' and James II decided the succession to the throne of England three hundred years ago.

The valley's catchment basin has the advantage of providing a selection of first-class monuments which give us a wonderful cross-section of Irish prehistory and history. For the historic period, this can easily be experienced at sites like Monasterboice, Mellifont and Trim, which are treated separately in this guide. But the core of the valley also provides us with the most famous cluster of prehistoric tombs — Newgrange, Knowth and Dowth.

All three tombs are large man-made mounds, with a passage leading from the edge into a central tomb — or two in the case of Knowth. The same idea, though differing in shape, permeates the Egyptian pyramids which, however, were probably built about 500 years later.

Newgrange, of course, has become internationally known, too, as the scene of the rising sun on mid-winter day penetrating into the very centre of the tomb, showing the living and the dead that, as in nature's annual cycle, there is a new beginning after the darkness of death is passed.

This group of tombs, and the satellite monuments in their closer and more distant environs, make the Boyne Valley seem like a sacred sanctuary which continues to attract devotees down to the present day.

Newgrange Tumulus
Open daily mid-March to May 10.00–13.00 hours and 14.00–17.00 hours.
Open daily June to mid-September 10.00–19.00 hours. Last tour at 18.30 hours.
Open daily mid-September to October 10.00–13.00 hours and 14.00–17.00 hours.
Tuesday to Sunday November to mid-March 10.00–13.00 hours and 14.00–16.30 hours.
Enquiries phone (041) 24488.
Literature available at site.

MEATH

Fourknocks/passage-tomb
O11 62

Although Newgrange, Knowth and Dowth are the most famous passage-tombs in Meath, the county has many others either in groups, as at Loughcrew below (p. 146), or isolated, as in the case of Fourknocks.

The builders of Fourknocks chose a typical hill-top site, so that the tomb would be visible for many miles around. Like the Boyne valley tombs above, it also consists of a man-made mound with a central tomb-chamber entered through a passage, but it differs considerably from them in that the tomb-chamber at Fourknocks occupies much more of the total area of the mound, as do similar tombs in Portugal. Another difference is that, in this instance, the man-made mound is modern, covering an ingeniously-constructed concrete dome built to protect and to preserve the tomb, which has helped to recreate much of the mysterious atmosphere which Stone Age man must have felt on entering the cavernous tomb-chamber when it was first built some 5,000 years ago.

Passage-tombs occur in innumerable variations along the whole Atlantic coastline of Europe from southern Spain to Scandinavia, but it may well be that those people buried at Fourknocks were not seafarers from so far afield, but indigenous stock who had settled in Ireland many hundreds, if not thousands, of years before.

MEATH

Kells/High Crosses/Round Tower/St Columb's House
N74 76

The town of Kells in Co. Meath is most famous for the book which bears its name, and which is now the greatest treasure in the library of Trinity College, Dublin — the *Book of Kells*. The book once belonged to, and may well have actually been written in, the old monastery which once flourished here.

The monastery came into being when the monks fled from St Columba's foundation at Iona after the Vikings had twice attacked it in the first decade of the 9th century. Part of the street pattern of the modern town reflects the original circular shape of the old monastery, at the centre of which was the church from which the famous book was temporarily removed in 1006. In its place stands a much more modern Church of Ireland structure, which has an interesting historical display on its balcony.

Surviving from the ancient monastery are a

*Passage-tombs
Loughcrew*

Round Tower, St Columb's House — in reality a
stone-roofed church building — and four High
Crosses which represent the most significant
collection of these typically Irish monuments
anywhere in the country.

Three of these are in the Church of Ireland
grounds: one, beside the Round Tower, has an
inscription dedicating it to SS Patrick and
Columba; a second is unfinished, while a third
must have been one of the largest and most
impressive of all, to judge by the base and shaft
which is all that survives.

The fourth cross, the so-called Market Cross,* is
located at a road junction in the town.

*Not in the care of the Office of Public Works.

MEATH

Loughcrew/passage-tombs
N57–60 77/78

The stone cairns of Loughcrew are on the summits
of three neighbouring hills — Carnbane West,
Carnbane East and Patrickstown — south-east of
Oldcastle. The hill gets its Irish name, Sliabh na
Cailligh [the Hill of the Witch], from a local
tradition which recalls that the witch created the
mounds by dropping stones out of her apron.

These mounds, thirty-two in number but
probably more originally, are none other than one
of the most imposing collections of Irish passage-
tombs of around 3000 BC, belonging to the same

family as the better-known examples of Newgrange, Knowth and Dowth (see p. 144 above), which lie about thirty-five miles further to the east in the same county.

Like the Boyne valley tombs, the cemetery has larger passage-tombs on the top of each hill, and smaller ones clustered around them. Like the Boyne valley examples, too, many of them are decorated with geometrical motifs, spirals, zigzags and, among others, what may be taken to be the rayed sun. The purpose of these designs is uncertain, though they may reflect ornament which decorated the walls of the houses of the tomb-builders in order to make the dead 'feel at home'.

The Loughcrew tombs were studied in the 1850s and 1860s by the local teacher, Eugene Conwell, and the distinguishing letters he gave them have been retained in their modern nomenclature. Conwell and others carried out rather inadequate excavations in the last century, but only one, Cairn H, has been excavated in this century, providing evidence that, during the Iron Age, a workshop in it was decorating animal bones with typically Celtic ornament.

MEATH

Tara/royal site
N92 60

Those accustomed to seeing this famous Co. Meath hill through the rose-tinted spectacles of 'The Harp that once through Tara's Halls' may be sorely disappointed to find neither halls nor walls, and to discover instead that this humped ridge, which gives a panoramic view over seven counties, seems to have little more to offer than a few mounds of earth, signifying nothing to the uninitiated. But armed with historical information and imagination the site can be brought to life as one of the most significant cult and power centres of early Ireland.

Already sanctified 4,000 years ago by those who built a passage-tomb known as 'The Mound of the Hostages', it once more played an important role when, in the early centuries after Christ, it acted as the nursery of power for the Uí Néill, a dynasty apparently of Connacht origin, which was to use this as a base to gain hegemony over much of the northern half of Ireland during the second half of AD first millennium.

According to legend, it was one of their druids who fought unsuccessfully against the introduction of Christianity by St Patrick. Before St Patrick's day, the Uí Néill had settled in one of the round earthworks — the Rath of the Synods, which excavations showed to belong to around AD 3rd century. But there are also other similar earthworks on the hill — the 'Forradh' and 'Cormac's House' — in the centre of which is the Lia Fáil [the Stone of Destiny], on which the kings were crowned. They also demonstrate some form of settlement. However, legend envisages the site as having already been abandoned on a permanent basis in AD 6th century, when it and its inhabitants were cursed by St Ruadhán of Lorrha.

That it was originally more of a cult centre than a fortification is suggested by the hill's being largely surrounded by a bank with a ditch *inside* it, rather than outside. But what is normally interpreted as the 'Banqueting Hall' where Thomas Moore imagined the harp being plucked, may be nothing of the sort, but a ceremonial entrance for men and horses leading from the main roads of Ireland into what, for centuries, remained as the imagined permanent seat of power of the High Kings of Ireland.

MEATH

Trim/castle and medieval monuments
N80–81 57

Trim Castle, which is situated on the south side of the River Boyne, is the largest Anglo-Norman fortress in Ireland. Its curtain walls enclose an area of over three acres and almost in the centre of the ward stands a most impressive isolated keep which is basically square in plan with four projecting

Trim Castle

towers. The Castle was built by Walter de Lacy in a least two phases, the first *c.* 1200 and the second being completed by 1220. The earlier structures consist of the lower portion of the keep and the gatehouse and square towers of the northern half of the monument. The D-shaped curtain towers, the gatehouse and barbican at the south side belong to the later period. A rock cut moat outside the curtain walls was fed with water from the river. The earliest fortification here was erected by Hugh de Lacy in 1170 and part of the remains of its ditch can be seen around the keep.

Walter de Lacy died in 1241 and his lands were divided between his grand-daughters Matilda and Margaret. Matilda married Geoffrey de Geneville, a French Nobleman in the service of the King c.1252. Matilda died in 1302 and in 1307 Geoffrey gave the Castle and lands to his grand-daughter Joan who had married Roger de Mortimer. During the Bruce invasion in 1315 de Mortimer fled from the Scots at Kells, Co. Meath. In 1316 a grant was made to him "to hold all the lands held by him directly and forfeited by reason of his tenants' revolt in the Scottish War".

Clonmacnois monastic remains

From the archaeological evidence, it would appear that the Castle ceased to be a residence after the middle of the 14th Century at which time it was in the hands of Roger de Mortimer, grandson of Joan and Roger.

OFFALY

Clonmacnois/old Irish monastery
N01 31

Clonmacnois is the very epitome of the early Irish monastery, combining a number of stone monuments so typical of these great

*Castledermot
High Cross*

establishments which earned for Ireland the title of 'Island of Saints and Scholars'. It boasts two Round Towers, one of which is incorporated into one of the six surviving churches, and also two complete and other fragmentary High Crosses. Of these, the most famous is the Cross of the Scriptures, which gets its name from the many biblical scenes, including *The Crucifixion* and *The Last Judgment*, carved upon it.

The planned Interpretative Centre will explain the site's vivid history from the time of its foundation by St. Kieran around 545-548 to the time when it was sacked and despoiled by the English in 1552. The monastery's present peaceful location on the banks of the Shannon River gives little indication of the throngs of monks who once lived there, and who made it one of the most important artistic centres of early Ireland.

In medieval times, the centre of veneration was the tomb of the founding saint, who lies buried here at what was once the centre of Ireland, where the main east-west roadway crossed the main north-south traffic artery of early Ireland — the River Shannon, which still brings many visitors by boat. But it was a helicopter which brought Clonmacnois its most famous pilgrim-visitor — Pope John Paul II — who visited the site in 1979.

Open daily November to mid-March 10.00–17.00 hours.
Daily mid-March to mid-May 10.00–18.00 hours.
Daily mid-May to early September 9.00–19.00 hours.
Daily September to October 10.00–18.00 hours.
Enquiries phone (0905) 74195.
Literature available at site.

KILDARE

Castledermot/monastic remains
S78 85

The original name of this holy spot was Dísert Diarmata, an isolated hermitage [Latin: *desertum*] occupied by the anchorite Diarmait (825), and which later became a monastic centre. He was associated with the famous religious reform movement of the Culdees, or *Céilí Dé* [servants of God] whose main centres of asceticism were the monasteries of Tallaght and Finglas — now both in the suburbs of Dublin — and Terryglass in Co. Tipperary. His tomb may have been close to the present Church of Ireland church, marked perhaps by a hump-backed cross-decorated stone unique in Ireland, but with close analogues in northern England.

This curious monument lies between two attractive 9th-century High Crosses, each bearing a *Crucifixion* scene, representations of the *Apostles, Adam and Eve* and, on the bases, scenes of *The Multiplication of the Loaves and Fishes*. The figures on both crosses are slightly stiff because they are carved from intractable granite, the same bright and glistening stone from which the somewhat later Round Tower and Romanesque door-fragment, standing nearby, are also made.

Not even the force of the Norman invasion could quash the sanctity of the place, as evidenced by the presence of a Franciscan friary church of 13th- and 14th-century date, and the St. John's Tower, a remnant of a 13th-century monastery of Crutched Friars.

KILDARE

Maynooth/Castle
N94 38

To the right of the entrance of St Patrick's College, now a university, in Maynooth, is a strong castle which was for long the power-centre of one of Ireland's great Anglo-Norman families, the Fitzgeralds, whose titles over the years included Earls and Marquesses of Kildare, and Dukes of Leinster. It was the ancestor of the family, Gerald Fitzmaurice, 1st Baron Offaly, who died in 1203, who built the first castle on the site, but the present stout keep was probably erected by one of his descendants during the course of the 13th century. The gatehouse and great hall, however, are probably later accretions.

The 8th and 9th Earls, Garret Mór and Garret Óg, who were virtually uncrowned kings of Ireland in the late 15th and early 16th centuries, built up a great library of manuscripts and early printed books here. But the castle was taken by Henry VIII's deputy, Sir William Skeffington, in 1535, and it served for a while as the Lord Deputy's residence before being returned to the Earls of Kildare in 1552. Re-edified in 1630, it was dismantled by order of Owen Roe O'Neill in 1647, and subsequently abandoned.

The manorial church* was incorporated into the nearby Church of Ireland church.

*Not in the care of the Office of Public Works.

WICKLOW

Glendalough/early monastery
T12 96

Glendalough, tucked away in the Wicklow Hills, is a valley of two lakes, and a monastery of two saints. The later of the pair of saints was Laurence O'Toole — one of the few Irish saints to have been formally canonised by the Pope in Rome.

Before he became Archbishop of Dublin in the 12th century, he was an abbot and builder of churches here, including probably St Saviour's priory, now enveloped by a tree plantation in the valley floor. But it is the earlier of the two — St Kevin —whom we most associate with Glendalough, for he was the inspiration for the monastic foundation which expanded around his tomb after his death in 618, allegedly at the biblical age of 120.

The monastery had two foci, one at each of the two lakes in the valley. The upper one is simpler and more austere than the lower one, evocative of the hermitical side of St Kevin's nature, where woods and water provide the setting for Reefert Church, within whose walls sleep many Leinster kings.

The lower centre houses the major monuments — one of Ireland's best-loved Round Towers, the roofless cathedral, a stone-roofed church with

miniature Round Tower [St Kevin's Kitchen], and the diminutive Priest's House, which is probably the saint's tomb-shrine, built in the 12th century.

This most romantic of monastic sites was one of Ireland's greatest pilgrimage centres up to the middle of the 19th century, and its story is told in sound and pictures in the imaginatively-designed new Interpretative Centre, where the Romanesque Market Cross and a large model of the monastery are also fittingly displayed.

Open daily mid-March to mid-June 10.00–17.00 hours.
Daily mid-June to mid-September 10.00–19.00 hours.
Daily mid-September to October 10.00–17.00 hours.
Tuesday to Saturday November to mid-March 10.00–16.30 hours. Sunday 13.30–16.30 hours.
Enquiries phone (0404) 5325/5352.
Literature available at site.

WICKLOW

Rathgall/stone fort
S*90 73*

The granite lands of south-west Wicklow preserve one monument which is impressive both for itself and for what it was found to contain through excavation. This is Rathgall [the Bright Fort, or Fort of the Foreigners], which has a total of three concentric walls spaced at various distances apart. The innermost one is purely of stone, and may be as late as the medieval period. The outer two — made of earth, but with some stone facing, still surviving — are earlier, but how much earlier is difficult to say.

Though stone forts are quite numerous in other parts of the country, what makes Rathgall unique is what the archaeologist's spade unearthed during the 1960s.

Firstly, there was the discovery of three Late Bronze Age cremated burials of around the 7th century BC — the first of their kind to have come

to light in Ireland. Hundreds of closely-spaced holes found nearby were considered to have held wooden stakes for the funeral pyre.

Secondly, and more importantly, was the finding of a timber structure which turned out to be the only known workshop of an Irish bronzesmith of the same period. The 400 or so fragments of clay moulds show that he was occupied in producing swords and spearheads made of bronze.

LAOIS

Killeshin/Romanesque church
S*67 78*

Although in Co. Laois, Killeshin is only a few miles from Carlow town, in a valley which once bore the name Glen Unshin. An early monastery on the site was probably founded by a St Comghán, whose name has curiously been virtually forgotten ages ago in the neighbourhood.

What still stays very much in the memory, however, is the later 12th-century west doorway of the surviving church, with a colourful interplay of reddish and pinkish sandstone which, centuries later, the Venetians were to use to perfection. Not even the weathering, which has taken its toll of the ornament, can prevent us from admiring the capitals bearing bearded and clean-shaven human heads, with hair blossoming out into foliage, or animals; or the virtuoso carving of the arches with zigzag, floral, animals and cross-diaper patterns; or the splendid bearded head which dominates the whole doorway from his lofty perch at the top of the outermost arch. The bulbous bases and the tall — partially-restored — gable would suggest a date in the second half of the 12th century, and it is sad that the fragmentary inscription on the abacus above the capitals of the doorway can no longer be deciphered satisfactorily, as it might have given us the name of a Leinster king who had been involved in building the church.

Not far from the church was a Round Tower, which was destroyed in 1703.

Glendalough monastic remains

Killeshin,
Romanesque Doorway

Fore Abbey

LAOIS

Timahoe/Round Tower
S54 90

Timahoe's main claim to fame is in having, what is probably, the most decorative Round Tower in Ireland. Situated in a broad and fertile valley, it gets its name Teach Mochua, or Mochua's House, from a saint who died around 655.

The Round Tower is about 29.60 high, including the re-built conical cap, and its walls are amongst the thickest of any Irish Round Tower. Its main attraction is the doorway in the Romanesque style which seems to have been part of the original structure, thus dating the tower to the 12th century. The doorway, best studied with a pair of binoculars as its base is 4.78 m above ground, stands out in relief from the wall surface, and is stepped up within to give access to the interior, which once had four storeys above it, originally reached by a series of wooden ladders which no longer exist.

The doorway itself is decorated with typical Romanesque bearded heads on both bases and capitals, those on the latter having hair which intertwines with that of the neighbouring head. The lowest window, with a pediment, also bears Romanesque heads.

Round Towers are found only on ecclesiastical sites, and although often considered to have been built as refuges for the monks against the Vikings, or their own Irish neighbours, they are more likely to have served purely religious purposes, such as the treasure-house of the monastery's relics, direct access to which could have been purposely prevented by having the doorway well above ground level.

Close to the Round Tower are the remains of a large early church with a blocked up chancel arch and remains of a tower added in the 15th century.

WESTMEATH

Fore/early church and Benedictine abbey
N51 70

Even without the 'Seven Wonders' (such as water flowing uphill) which local tradition associates with Fore, the place is wonderful in itself.

Fore is located in a valley running east-west 1.25 km (two miles) from Castlepollard, and would be special —if for nothing else — for the strength of the water which wells up out of the ground on the valley floor. It is dedicated to the saint who made Fore famous — St Feichín, an ascetic monk who died from the Yellow Plague in 664, when the monastery he had founded there is said to have numbered already 300 monks.

The church, placed on the terrace above the powerful well, was built probably many centuries later. Its most distinguishing feature is the 2.5 tonnes lintel above the door, with cross-decoration both inside and out. The chancel is a secondary addition of around 1200, and the arch was rebuilt by the Office of Public Works in 1934.

Above the church is the so-called 'Anchorite's Cell', now changed out of all recognition into a family mausoleum. From the well beside the road, a new path leads past a holy tree to the abbey — the only certainly-identified surviving monastery buildings in medieval Ireland of that great monastic order, the Benedictines.

The church itself is unusual in having towers at both ends. On a small hillock to the north-east is a fragmentary columbarium, or dove-cot, which helped to provide the monks with the main ingredient for their pigeon pies.

Though now a small village, Fore was once a fortified town in medieval times, to which the imposing gates at either end of the village still bear witness.

LONGFORD

Granard/motte
N33 81

Dominating the southern end of the town of Granard is a large mound of earth looking like an apple-dumpling bowl turned upside down. This is perhaps Ireland's most impressive example of a kind of earthwork known as a motte. These were erected by the early Norman invaders in the last few decades of the 12th century to establish a bridge-head with which to hold the land that they had so recently conquered by the sword, but before they had the time and the man-power to build the stone castles which were to follow early in the following century.

Granard motte is no exception to the general rule in having a flat top and, like the others, it would have had on top of it a wooden tower, known as a bretasche, or brattice, which would have served essentially the purpose of a look-out tower. Attached to this example, as also to many others, was a flat, sometimes half-moon-shaped area, known as a bailey, which was defended by a bank and ditch, and which served to keep cattle in at night. It would also have contained wooden residential buildings and a wooden hall which, like the bretasche, have long-since disappeared.

Wildlife

KILDARE

Pollardstown Fen
N77 16

Pollardstown Fen, with an area of approximately 220 hectares, is by far the longest of the spring-fed fens in Ireland. Some 12,000 years ago it was a large shallow lake — the margins of which were colonised by swamp and fen plants. Waterlogged conditions prevented the decomposition of these plants and, as a result, there began an accumulation of partly decomposed material which we now call peat or turf. At the same time, lime was being precipitated out of the very calcareous spring water wherever open water conditions prevailed. Finally, the lake was overgrown and became dominated by swamps and fen plants. The vegetation is quite varied and species-rich, with twenty-one communities and six rare or uncommon species.

Fauna range from a diversity of invertebrates to a variety of waterfowl and other birds.

The fen is part of the water supply to the Grand Canal. (See Inland Waterways below, pp. 162, 181.) Access is via the canal banks at Milltown at the west end, or beside the gravel works at the east end.

Visitors are welcome but, because of dangeous ground conditions, they should adhere to the pathway leading to the fen.

LAOIS

Coolacurragh Wood
S35 80

This wood is exactly like that described in

Grantstown Wood below and it too has an ecosystem which is extremely rare in Ireland today.

Both woods are accessible at all times, but there are no visitor services.

LAOIS

Grantsown Wood and Lough
S33 58

This reserve is situated about 8 km west-north-west of Durrow in Co. Laois, as is Coolacurragh Wood above. It is a rare example of wet woodland on base-rich soils, while Grantsown Lough is a classic example of a lake which has gradually infilled through fen to alder carr.

Native woodland species dominate the woodland, while an abundance of dead and decaying wood is of considerable conservation value.

LAOIS

Timahoe Esker
S54 92

This ridge is 1 km north-east of Timahoe, Co. Laois, and it is one of the few esker ridges left in the country which still carries native woodland. Although extensively planted with conifers and other exotic species, it is planned to expand the native woodland, using appropriate management techniques.

It is accessible at all times but care should be exercised in the event of timber felling. There are no visitor services.

*Pollardstown Fen
Co. Kildare*

LAOIS/OFFALY

Slieve Bloom Mountains
N25 10

The summits of these mountains are covered in well-developed blanket bog with a luxuriant growth of *Sphagna*, lichens and heathers. The area contains the headwaters of several major rivers.

It is accessible at all times via several roads and tracks crossing the hills. Visitors are advised to adhere to these as parts of the bogland are very soft and unsafe.

OFFALY

Clara Bog
N25 30

This is a raised bog situated 2 km south of Clara

town in north Co. Offaly. It is of international importance as one of the largest relatively intact bogs of its type remaining in Ireland.

A feature of outstanding significance is its well-developed 'soak' system widely regarded as the best in Western Europe. Soaks are internal drainage systems found in large raised bogs where, due to surface run-off or springs, increased water-flow allows more nutrient demanding species to exist. It is probable that the springs draw their water supply from the large esker which lies

Soak system at Clara Bog, Co. Offaly

between Clara town and the bog.

Clara possesses the full range of physical features and species associated with normal raised bogs. There are bog pools, hummock/hollow complexes, moss 'lawns' and, along the northern margin, relatively undisturbed transitions to mineral soils.

Bog mosses [*Sphagnum* species] thrive in the acid nutrient poor conditions and form the substratum in which grow insect-eating plants, like sundews [*Drosera* species] and efficient nutrient recyclers, such as heathers, bog cotton and bog rosemary.

Merlins hunt along the bog margins while red grouse and the Irish hare graze the heathers.

The bog can be viewed from the public road. It is unsafe for general access.

OFFALY

Raheenmore Bog
N44 32

The bog is situated 7 km north-west of Daingean, Co. Offaly, and it is a classic example of raised bog in a deep basin. It has a well-developed dome with typical raised bog vegetation.

There is no public access to this bog which is too soft and unsafe for visitors.

WICKLOW

Deputy's Pass
T59 92

The pass is near Glenealy in Co. Wicklow. Although coppice in origin, it is a good example of Wicklow oak woodland. As the region was formerly planted for forestry, a considerable amount of work remains to be done on this area by way of eliminating exotic, non-native tree species, especially conifers.

It is accessible at all times and it has a good road system.

Glendalough
T11 94

Glendalough is famous for its scenery and its association with an ancient ecclesiastical settlement. Part of its beauty lies in native woodland comprised mainly of sessile oak — a remnant of the primeval forest which, in prehistoric times, covered the greater part of Ireland.

These woods give some indication of vegetation as it was when St Kevin founded his monastery some fourteen centuries ago. The oaks here are the direct descendants of those which occupied the valley in that time. Charcoal hearths are still identifiable in the woods, dating from the iron-smelting period which continued into the 17th century, when charcoal from the coppiced oak was used to smelt the local bog iron-ore.

Glenealo Valley
T11 96

Glenealo nature reserve adjoining Glendalough includes the Upper Lake, the origin of which dates back to glacial times, together with adjoining broad open valley and surrounding mountains where the vegetation is representative of typical Wicklow Mountain variety. The area supports a good population of wild deer.

Glendalough and Glenealo Valley are accessible at all times. Both nature reserves will form part of a national park which is being established in the Wicklow Mountains.

An information office near Glendalough's Upper Lake will open during 1990 and nature trails through the reserves will commence from there. Information is also available at National Monuments' interpretative centre nearby (see pp. 151–2).

Glen of the Downs
T26 11

This glen is about 8 km south of Bray in Co. Wicklow on the main Dublin to Wexford road. It is an area of sessile oak and it is a very good example of the dryer type of oakwood characteristic of acid soils in Wicklow.

It is accessible at all times and it has a picnic area.

Vale of Clara
T18 90

This reserve comprises a large area of fragmented oakwood mostly on the eastern side of the Avonmore River. It contains the largest area of semi-natural woodlands in Co. Wicklow and it is potentially one of the biggest stands of native hardwoods in the country. The area has been at least partially under woodland since the last Ice Age. The oakwoods are also of high scenic value.

The vale is accessible at all times but there are no visitor services.

Rabbit

SLIGO
Lower Lough Erne
Upper Lough Erne
Lough Allen
Ballinamore and
Ballyconnell Canal
Clondra
Mullingar
Lough Ree
The Royal Canal
ATHLONE
The Grand Canal
Shannon Harbour
DUBLIN
NAAS
The Barrow Navigation
NEW ROSS
The Shannon Navigation
Shannon
GALWAY
Lough Derg
LIMERICK

DUNDALK

Lower Lough Erne
Upper Lough Erne
Ballinamore and
Ballyconnell Canal
Lough Allen
Leitrim
Carrick-on-Shannon
Jamestown
Albert Lock
Dromod
Roosky Lock
Carnadoe Waters
Lough Forbes
Tarmonbarry Lock
Clondra
Lough Key
Boyle
SLIGO

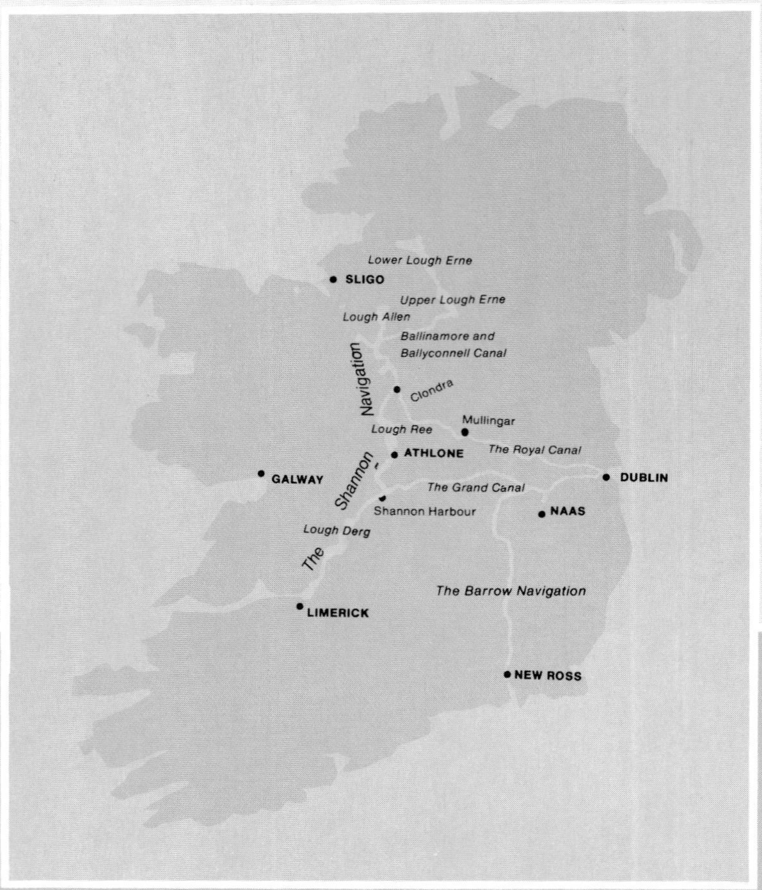

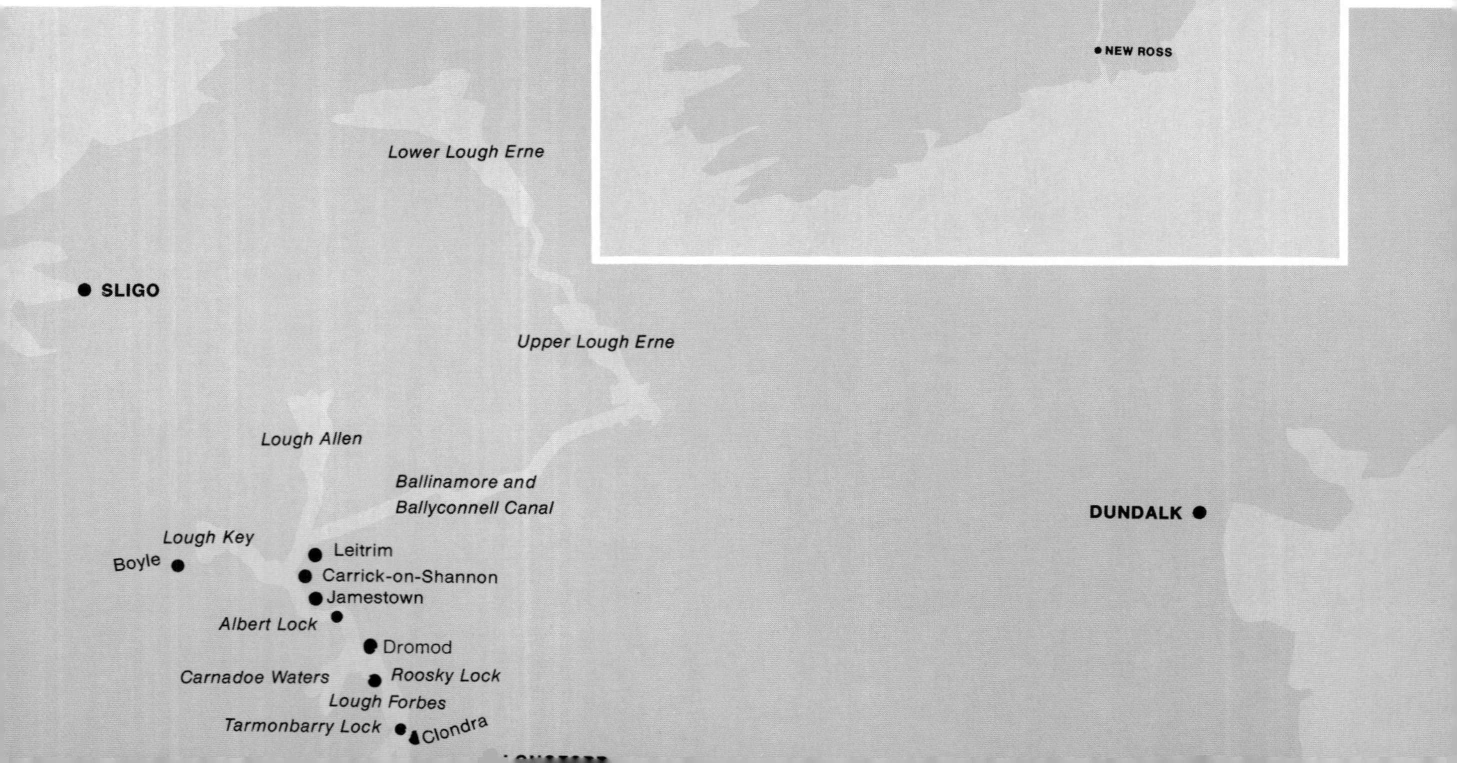

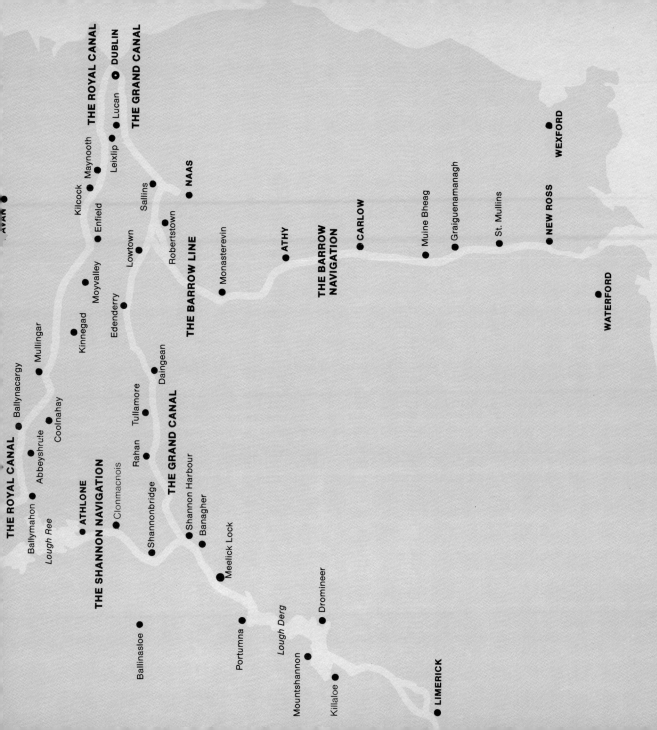

Inland Waterways

While the commercial life of the waterways could be considered ended, a whole new future is opening up for this remarkable national heritage. The Office of Public Works now controls over 563 km (350 miles) of navigable waterways, as well as the large cruising areas of the Shannon lakes, together with a further 160 km (100 miles) of navigations which are under reconstruction or can be restored.

HISTORICAL BACKGROUND

The Canal Age

The story behind the rich heritage of inland waterways in Ireland began in the mid-1700s. At that time the Canal Age had begun in Europe but the first watershed canal in these islands — the Newry Canal — linking Lough Neagh with the Irish Sea at Newry, was completed in 1742. In the years that followed Ireland gained a waterway network far in excess of that warranted by the amount of inland trade in the country at that time. The expectation that the improved transport system would encourage industrial development did not materialise.

The Railway Age

Just when the waterways were beginning to show some small profits, the Railway Age arrived. The faster transport offered by rail killed the waterborne passenger trade very quickly and a war of rates developed for the commercial trade. The waterways, struggling to compete for this trade with the railways, received a further setback in the 1940s with a new form of competition — road transport.

The late 1940s and early 1950s were the darkest years for inland waterways in Ireland. Commercial traffic had reached a low ebb, resulting in a number of waterways falling into disuse and having to be closed. In Northern Ireland, during this period, some of the navigations were completely abandoned, or absorbed in road works, and the task of restoration would be almost impossible. In the rest of Ireland closures were more limited but the revival of interest in waterways — because of their tourist potential and amenity value — has come just in time.

MUCH TO SEE AND TO DO

What's on offer?

Ireland's waterways have much to offer to those seeking something different in the way of a holiday, whether it be a journey into the past along the quiet waters of the Grand Canal, a trip down the picturesque River Barrow or a holiday on the Shannon River with its varied scenery, its interesting historic sites and its tempting waters.

So, whether your interest is in bird-life, flora, fauna, fishing or archaeology, or if you are just in search of tranquillity, the waterways will fulfil your needs. They carve out silvery routes through Ireland's green countryside, which in some cases are rivers which have been used by people from early times, and in others are man-made canals, lines of communication which, over the years, have become part of the natural environment and have created their own water-based habitat.

Ways to see and to use the waterways

There are many and varied ways to see the

waterways. A good modern cruising fleet is available for those who wish to hire with a choice of about 450 well-equipped boats from which to choose. Experience in handling a boat is an advantage, but is not a necessity. A holiday on the canals is a good way to begin if you are not used to boating, but there are many who have coped successfully with a first-time holiday on the Shannon.

If you prefer a sailing holiday there are boats for hire on Lough Derg and a pleasant week of good sailing can be enjoyed on its extensive waters, or you can hire a sailing dinghy with your cruiser. For those who want to go afloat, but are not confident enough to manage a boat of their own, there are a number of firms providing floating holidays on the Shannon with everything laid on. Bord Fáilte at Baggot Street Bridge in Dublin 2 can supply information about all these firms and their rates.

You may decide to bring your own boat onto the waterways and, if so, there are many good access slips or you can enter from the sea at Dublin, Limerick and the Waterford Estuary. There are a number of marinas where private boats can be moored for short, or long, stays. You may decide to undertake a canoe trip and this is an ideal way to visit the waterways and even to penetrate further

Grand Canal at Portobello from an old engraving

163

up the headwaters.

The Office of Public Works is very conscious of the many ways in which you can enjoy the waterways and they are committed to making linear parks of them for the enjoyment of all. There is excellent bank fishing in many places. The canals and the River Barrow offer interesting walking routes along towpaths. However, it is advisable to arm yourself with a guide to the waterway to find out the road approaches and the best side on which to walk.

Fishing

The Shannon is a paradise for fishermen, offering a great variety of fishing from fast flowing waters to tranquil ones around the reed-lined shores of

*Fishing on the
River Shannon*

the lakes. Because many parts of the river are inaccessible except by boat, these waters are seldom fished. Many specimens have been caught in the Shannon and a wide variety of fish are found. The guide books offer detailed information as to the best places to fish and how to catch different species. In addition, local people are helpful about sharing their secrets.

The Grand Canal and Royal Canal, although man-made, have over the passage of time established almost natural aquatic ecosystems. The reed fringes along the edges of the waterway provide a habitat for a wide diversity of aquatic insects on which the fish feed. They also oxygenate the water during the daylight hours and offer fish shelter from bright sunlight and cover from predators.

The Office of Public Works is very much aware that the true angling potential of the waterways has yet to be realised and optimising this potential has now become an important element in the overall development plans which see the waterways as multi-purpose amenity areas. The canals already hold big stocks of bream, rudd, rudd/bream hybrids, tench, perch, eels and some roach and pike — pike up to 9.08 kg (20 lbs) have been caught on the Grand Canal.

Some areas are already established as excellent fishing grounds and government funding to the Office of Public Works and the Central Fishery Board, specifically to encourage the establishment of the canals as a coarse angling fishery, will enable a major re-stocking programme to be carried out, conservation to be maintained and further fishing stands to be established.

So, as you journey through the countryside, be aware of the waterways, stop and look at them and enjoy their special environment. They are an important part of our birthright and one that we very nearly lost.

THE RIVER SHANNON

The Shannon Navigation offers 258 km (160

Lough Key

miles) of cruising waterway but, because of the lakes along its course, there is a total of more than 2,000 sq. km (80 sq. miles) of cruising grounds to explore. There are very few locks — only six from Lough Key on the Boyle Waters to Killaloe at the southern end of Lough Derg. With no commercial and light holiday traffic, there is nothing to disturb the tranquil atmosphere. When the proposed re-opening of the Shannon-Erne link, the Ballinamore and Ballyconnell Canal, takes place, Ireland will have a cruising ground unrivalled in Europe.

Its Historical Background

The Shannon has always played an important and strategic role in Irish history, providing an easy means of communication through the heart of the country in the days before a road network had been established. The Vikings penetrated as far upstream as Lough Ree, dragging their longships up the rapids, and Irish chieftains struggled for control of its waters against both the Vikings and each other.

*Knockvicar Bridge,
Boyle Waters*

*Oakport Lake,
Boyle Waters*

A number of important monastic settlements were established on sites along its course and the remains of these are among some of the finest in Europe. Later the river was used as a line of defence, cutting off the west from the east, and elaborate fortifications were erected at some crossing places, at a time when an invasion by Napoleon's French forces from the west was feared.

Shannon Navigation

The first attempts to improve the navigation were made in the 1750s and, when the new Office of Public Works was set up in 1831, the Shannon Navigation was transferred to them and it has been under their administration ever since. The early works, however, were not very satisfactory and they were virtually reconstructed in the 1840s when the arrival of steam-driven boats on the river overcame the need for towpaths.

The large locks were constructed to accommodate the steamers which, in fact, did not continue to operate for very long. The same steam power, which had brought about the improved navigation works, also heralded the arrival of the Railway Age which killed the passenger traffic and curtailed the development of commercial trade.

By the early 1960s, when all commercial traffic on the Grand Canal had ceased, there was virtually no movement on the river, and the newly-formed Inland Waterways Association of Ireland had to fight hard to prevent its total strangulation, when some of the Local Authorities sought to replace the old opening bridges with low fixed structures. But the tide was to turn: launches to take passengers for trips were placed on the river, firms offering boats for hire commenced trading and the number of privately-owned boats increased.

A whole new era was opening up for the Shannon Navigation and facilities were improved to cater for this new resurgence.

Upper Shannon and Boyle Waters

The riverside town of Carrick-on-Shannon is an ideal centre from which to explore the upper river and it has good shops, along with other facilities. From here you can cruise upstream to Lough Key, entering the Boyle Waters and passing through a number of delightful lakes on the way, and through the village of Cootehall, which has some well-known hostelries, before locking up into Lough Key itself. It is a picturesque lake with many wooded islands and a magnificent forest park with much to interest the visitor.

From the head of the navigation of the Boyle Waters at Drum Bridge it is only a 3 km (1.9 miles) walk into Boyle, which still portrays something of the atmosphere of an old coaching town, and contains the fascinating ruins of a 12th-century Cistercian abbey (see National Monuments above, page 102).

Retracing your course to the confluence of the Boyle Waters with the Shannon, you can follow the river to Battlebridge and enter the Lough Allen

Lough Allen Canal

Carrick-on-Shannon

Canal. This brings you to a delightful little lake, Acre Lake, close to Drumshanbo, which owes its origins to the iron-smelting business of past days and is now a busy little town with most facilities.

Jamestown to Lanesborough

Downstream from Carrick, the river makes a great loop which is by-passed by a short canal — the Jamestown Canal. The little villages of Jamestown and Drumsna are located a short distance along each arm of the loop. Because of the strategic importance of the fast flowing river as a defensive line, the land enclosed by the loop was a settled area in early times and a great embankment, the *dún*, or fortress, was constructed to protect the people inside from invaders.

The navigation passes through two large lakes, Boderg and Bofin, with an arm leading off Lough Boderg into the Carnadoe Waters. This is an enchanting place, with the navigation stealing through a series of reed-lined lakes connected by narrow, twisting channels. It is a wonderful spot for both the bird-watcher and the fisherman, a natural habitat for all kinds of water-loving plants and a haven for those who just want to 'get away from it all'.

The little village of Dromod in the north-east corner of Lough Bofin is served by two harbours, one dating from the 1820s and the other constructed in recent times with a tennis court nearby. At the southern end of Lough Bofin, the river passes through Roosky — a village with a good supermarket by the bridge and a number of traditional Irish pubs — before opening out again into another lake, Lough Forbes. This lake has bogland stretching away on the west shore and, on the east shore, is the densely wooded Castle Forbes estate.

Tarmonbarry is where the Royal Canal joined the Shannon and it is possible to lock up into the old basin at Richmond Harbour, to follow an alternative route along a smaller river — the Camlin — to re-join the Shannon at Lough Forbes. A wide, but shallow, stretch of river follows to Lanesborough, at the northern end of Lough Ree, where there are a number of eating places, including a floating restaurant. Here it is important to ensure that the weather is suitable for crossing the Lough and to travel in company with another boat if it is windy.

Middle Shannon
Lough Ree has a number of interesting places to visit, including Lecarrow, at the end of a short canal, and Iniscleraun with its ruins of the monastic settlement founded by St. Diarmaid. There are further interesting sites on other islands and a fine Norman castle at Rindown, where the lake narrows.

Lough Boderg at sunrise

Albert Lock, Jamestown Canal

At the southern end of the lake on the west shore is the new harbour of Hodson Bay alongside a hotel and, on the opposite shore, a series of small lakes — the Inner Lakes — open off the main lake, offering another area of reed-lined water which is a bird sanctuary and, once again, a fisherman's paradise. There are a number of marinas here — the SGS Marina offers hotel and other facilities.

Athlone was the principal crossing place of the Shannon from early times at one of the main routes from east to west across the country. Just upstream of the town, the Jolly Mariner marina has a good riverside restaurant and mooring facilities. The fine town quays provide easy access to shops and restaurants. An interesting museum is housed in the keep of Athlone Castle and a good local guide book offers a 'tourist trail' to follow around this historic old town.

The stretch of river between Athlone and Banagher enjoys worldwide recognition for its bird population and some of the last unworked bogs in the country. The eskers, left behind by the Ice Age, are a distinctive feature. One of two round towers at Clonmacnois is visible for some distance as the river winds its way towards this renowned monastic site (see National Monuments above, page 149).

The Office of Public Works who are in charge of the monastic remains at Clonmacnois (see National Monuments, page 150), have carried out considerable restoration and conservation work there, providing endless interest for visitors. There

Athlone

Cruising on the Inner Lakes — Lough Ree

Clonmacnois

are good mooring jetties in the area too, and it is important to leave lots of time to view the interesting ruins and to study the High Crosses of Clonmacnois.

The bridge at Shannonbridge dates back to the mid-1700s and there are good quays on which to pull in to visit the fortifications, which are a unique example of artillery fortifications of the Napoleonic period.

After this inspection a short walk to the top of the village is essential to quench one's thirst in a well-known pub!

The Grand Canal enters the Shannon some distance downstream at Shannon Harbour and it is well worth stopping at the jetty below the last lock and walking up along the towpath to visit the terminus of the canal.

There are a number of interesting places to see ashore at Banagher, including more fortifications and even a martello tower. It is possible to make a short trip by road from here to visit the medieval church of Clonfert, with its famous Irish Romanesque doorway, before continuing downstream through the large Victoria Lock at Meelick, where there are further fortifications, and then on to Portumna at the head of Lough Derg.

Lower Shannon
The town of Portumna is a short walk from the bridge and can also be approached from the Portumna Forest Park Harbour in the north west corner of Lough Derg.

From this harbour an inspection of Portumna Castle can be made. Built in the early 1600s, it is a unique example of the transitional style of architecture between the vertical tower houses so common around the country and the later manor houses (see National Monuments above, page 99). Efforts are being made to secure the castle, which was destroyed by fire in the early 1800s, to prevent further disintegration and deterioration. Nearby are the ruins of a Dominican Priory and there is a most interesting nature trail through the forest

park with an observation tower for bird-watching in the nature reserve on the lakeshore.

Lough Derg, like Lough Ree, can be dangerous to cross in windy weather but it does have quite a number of harbours: Terryglass, the winner of awards for its well-kept village; Kilgarvan, with an excellent restaurant; Rossmore on the west shore; Dromineer, the home of the Lough Derg Yacht Club, where there are good restaurants; Garrykennedy with its pub, which is famed for its traditional music sessions; Tuamgraney and Scarriff, up a short length of winding river; Williamstown, Mountshannon, a popular sailing centre with an attractive village, which is also an award winner, and Killaloe, at the southern end of the lake, which is well supplied with places to eat and where you must visit St Flannan's Cathedral.

This is the limit of navigation for the hire craft but it is possible to proceed downstream through the locks at Ardnacrusha power station to reach the sea at Limerick.

Shannonbridge

THE GRAND CANAL

The main line of the Grand Canal is 132 km (82 miles) long from Dublin to Shannon Harbour on the River Shannon with the Barrow Line, which starts near Robertstown, extending south for 45 km (28 miles) to meet the River Barrow at Athy. In addition, there is a short spur into Edenderry and another, 4.8 km (3 miles) from the main line near Sallins to Naas, was re-opened in 1987. From Athy the navigation enters the River Barrow and 64 km (40 miles) of river navigation lie ahead before reaching the tidewater at St Mullin's.

The canal rises steeply out of Dublin city but, from Lucan Bridge, there are twenty-four locks in the remaining 125 km (77 miles) journey to the Shannon, and nine locks from Lowtown down to the River Barrow at Athy, with twenty-three locks down the Barrow Navigation. Whether you travel in a boat or a canoe or walk the towpath, a journey along the canal today is not only a journey back in time, observing its many interesting features, but it is also an opportunity to enjoy its remarkable flora and fauna.

This man-made waterway has created for itself its own natural habitat over the years. Water-loving plants, birds and insects can be observed and the hedgerows along the line of the canal are full of interest for the nature lover and the photographer. Above all, as it wends its way across the centre of Ireland, the canal offers a route far removed from noisy modern roads. The towns and villages provide an opportunity to stop for provisions or to visit the local pub, or you can just decide to stop wherever you wish to enjoy the peace and quiet, or to indulge in a little coarse fishing.

Historical Background

This was one of the canals which was commenced during the canal-building years in the 1750s. When the works were taken over by a private company, the Grand Canal Company, in 1772, very little had been achieved and it was to take the company over thirty years to complete the works at an average cost of about £6,000 per mile, by which time a debt of over £1,000,000 had been incurred. Despite this, branches to Ballinasloe, Mountmellick and Kilbeggan were added in the 1820s and 1830s funded by government loans.

This was a colourful era for the canal with a large number of trade boats, hauled by horses, in

Lower Lough Derg

Mountshannon

Water sports in Grand Canal Basin at Ringsend, Dublin

operation and a busy schedule of passenger boats. A series of canal hotels had been built to provide accommodation for the passengers at each end of the canal and at Sallins, Robertstown and Tullamore along the route.

Dublin to the Twelfth Lock

The Grand Canal and the Royal Canal are important features of the city and county of Dublin. They encircle the old city area: the Grand Canal to the south of the River Liffey and the Royal Canal to the north of it. They provide attractive linear parks, a breath of fresh air with their water habitats, and are much used by the people of the city.

Ringsend, where the Grand Canal enters the River Liffey, is full of interest for the canal historian. The construction of these great basins in the 1790s was a considerable engineering feat and, although they are little used by shipping today, this whole area has been designated for development with the water becoming the focus of interest.

The canal passes what was once the old canal

hotel at Portobello, which has recently undergone a complete refurbishment. By the time it reaches the Lucan Road it is 16 km (10 miles) from Ringsend and the city has been left far behind. The stretch from the eleventh lock, at Clondalkin to the thirteenth lock near Lyons House, was the earliest part of the canal to be built and the decision to reduce its dimensions is responsible for the strange shaped locks. A short distance above the old mill at the twelfth lock at Lucan Road there is a little square two-storied lock-keeper's

house, which dates back to the 1750s, and similar houses still survive on some of the other waterways. Nearby are Gollierstown quarries from which the stone for the locks and bridges was hewn and transported away by water as the canal crept westwards.

The Thirteenth to the Sixteenth Lock
Leaving the city of Dublin behind, the Grand Canal weaves its way westwards along hedgerows of hawthorn in its own little world of water-loving

Sallins

flora and fauna. Lyons House, near the thirteenth lock, is now a centre for the Department of Agriculture in University College Dublin. Glimpses of this large stone mansion may be seen from the canal. Sallins is very much a canal-side village and was the site of the first canal hotel — now demolished.

There was considerable discussion as to what method should be used from here to cross the Liffey and the first scheme was to lock down into the river and up again, but eventually a site was selected a short distance upstream and a fine aqueduct was built — the Leinster Aqueduct. It is possible to drive across it and to follow the canal by car for some miles westwards.

The Naas Canal enters the main line near the aqueduct. This canal was built by a company that was subsequently taken over by the Grand Canal Company. It was closed to navigation in 1961 and re-opened to Naas in 1987. It is a very pretty stretch of waterway and well worth the detour to Naas Harbour. It can also be viewed from the road which runs alongside it.

The Summit Level

The levels between the sixteenth and eighteenth locks are very popular with fishermen and this is a very lovely section of the canal. Robertstown is a most attractive canal-side village, being fortunate in the local community, who have done a great deal in making use of their location on the canal and the old canal hotel building. They offer visitors trips into the past, journeying along the canal and partaking of an 18th-century meal in authentic surroundings.

Nearby, Lowtown has become an important boating-centre with a well-equipped marina and a base from which boats can be hired for a trip down the Barrow Navigation. This is the summit level of the canal with the Milltown Supply, the principal feeder of the canal, providing it with crystal clear waters. Here the canal linking with the River Barrow enters from the south.

Swans on Grand Canal at Inchicore, Dublin

Leinster Aqueduct

The Bog of Allen and Edenderry

By now the traveller will have become accustomed to the attractive cutstone hump-backed bridges, which are a distinctive feature of the canal. There is one close to the turf-burning power station at Allenwood, locally called 'Scow Bridge', which is a skew-bridge, requiring great skill in its construction. The canal passes along the northern edge of this vast region of bogland and close to the busy market town of Edenderry, which is serviced by a short spur canal.

It was an extremely difficult stretch of canal to construct, with early engineers failing to recognise the necessity for bog-drainage and allowing the land to settle before making the canal. It was constructed at too high a level and later engineers were beset with problems in securing the high, unstable embankments, only to have a major breach recurring in 1989.

A small aqueduct — the Blundell Aqueduct — carries the canal across the Edenderry road and is known locally as 'The Tunnel'. This is a 32-kilometre (20-mile) level without a lock and soon the bog is left behind and the familiar hedgerows

Robertstown

are set in motion again.

...h of canal. The
Rhode
...on its
...ing
...es
...outh
...st
...d
...nt

ridges to await removal to the power station, where it is blown at pressure into the furnaces.

Daingean was named Philipstown by the English administration in the reign of Philip and Mary when this whole area was 'planted' with settlers in the 16th century. It was the assize town — hence its fine courthouse, now the fire station, attributed to James Gandon, but this position was later usurped by neighbouring Tullamore and it declined in importance. It has now reverted to its Irish name and it is a popular stopover for supplies and a visit to the 'locals'.

The Grand Canal at Ballycommon

*The Grand Canal
at Shannon Harbour*

Daingean to Tullamore

At the end of the 32-km (20-mile) level, the branch
to Kilbeggan formerly entered the main line but it
is now closed to navigation. There is a steep drop
down into Tullamore through six locks in the
space of a few miles. Celtic Canal Cruisers' base is
halfway down this flight and boaters can be sure of
a friendly welcome here if help is required. There
is a wide and imposing approach to this busy
market town, the original home of 'Irish Mist' and
'Tullamore Dew' whiskey.

This was the terminus of the canal for some
years in the 1790s, while the route to the Shannon
was being investigated, and a fine harbour was
constructed which is now the central work depot
for the canal. The harbour is down a short spur
and worth the detour, although the fine harbour
warehouses and canal hotel en route to it have
sadly all been demolished.

Tullamore to Pollagh

Shra and Ballycowan castles, beside the canal to
the west of Tullamore, are good examples of the
Irish fortified house. Dating from the late 16th and
early 17th century, respectively, they illustrate the
troubled state of the country, while by this time,
across the water, attractive manor houses were
being built.

The Huband and Charleville Aqueducts carry
the canal over two small rivers. It is a great pity to
pass over any of these aqueducts without pulling
in to have a look at them from below. Rahan was
formerly one of the passenger boat stations on the
canal and the name of the pub here, The Thatch,
is an indication of its long history when it was a
thatched house. There is a little quay here making
it a difficult place to pass! To work up a thirst, a
short walk to inspect the ancient churches nearby,
is rewarding.

Pollagh to Shannon Harbour

The little village of Pollagh has been revitalised by the activity on the surrounding bogs. It is noticeable that this stretch of canal, although passing through bog, does not have the high embankments of the Edenderry stretch. Lessons had been learnt and, before construction commenced, the ground was prepared by careful drainage channels over the years.

The Macartney Aqueduct named, as are so many of the bridges, after prominent early directors of the Grand Canal Company, carries the canal over the Silver River, a tributary of the Brosna. The canal follows the Brosna valley all the way from Tullamore and at Belmont the river and

A typical hump-backed canal bridge

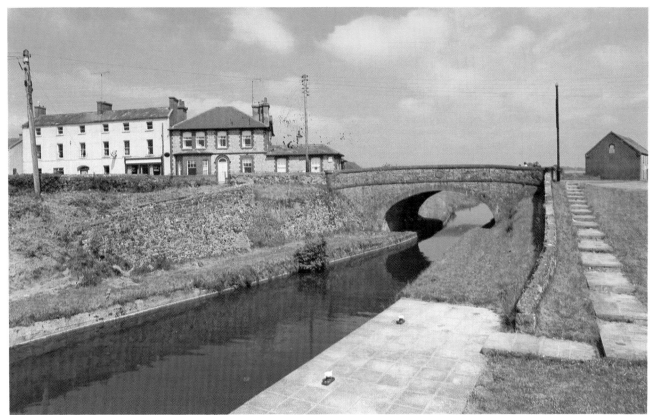

Daingean

181

The Grand Canal crossing the Bog of Allen

Levitstown Lock and old mill on the Barrow Navigation.

canal are only a short distance apart. Belmont mill stands beside the bridge over the Brosna, which has now become a sizeable river, soon to discharge into the River Shannon below Shannon Harbour, the terminus of the canal over a period of years.

More than any other place along the canal, Shannon Harbour evokes the past. The ruined hotel, the agent's house and other old buildings make it easy to picture the busy scene here in the 1820s, when crowds of emigrants made their way to this place, accompanied by grieving families, to embark on the first part of their long journey to a new life — or possible death — on the emigrant ship. At times the boat's captain had to call in the military to 'read the Riot Act' to prevent the wailing families from trying to board the boat to escort the emigrants part of the way.

Below the harbour the canal passes down through the thirty-fifth and thirty-sixth locks before entering the River Shannon. At one time

Vicarstown on the Barrow Line

the river was spanned here by a narrow wooden bridge which was used to bring the towing horses across to the Ballinasloe Canal. The bridge was subsequently replaced by a chain ferry which fell into disuse when the canal boats became mechanised.

Today the Ballinasloe Canal is gone. Much of it has disappeared in bog workings; in places the line of the towpath indicates its route and a light railway passes through one of its lock chambers. To re-open this canal would be out of the question, but moves are afoot to make the nearby River Suck navigable and so allow Ballinasloe to be reached by boat once more.

Barrow Line

Leaving the main line at Lowtown, near Robertstown, the Barrow Line follows the route of the River Slate around the Hill of Allen, traditionally associated with Fionn Mac Cool, a legendary Celtic hero, and on through Rathangan. The harbour and stores below the double lock here indicate that it was once a busy centre and much has been done to make this an inviting stopover place today.

The canal converges with the River Barrow as it approaches Monasterevan. Once a busy brewing and distilling town, it was also at one time the home of the famous tenor, John McCormack, who lived in Moore Abbey. The company had hoped to terminate the canal here and use the river navigation but it was decided to continue the stillwater canal to Athy because of shallows in the river. Originally boats had to lock down into the river and up again, but subsequently a very fine aqueduct was built to replace this laborious process. The enthusiast can seek out traces of the old locks and will also be fascinated by the lifting bridge, the first of a number of them to be encountered on the way south. The Mountmellick Canal joined the Grand Canal here but it was closed in 1960 and parts of it around Portarlington have been turned into a ring road.

Before reaching Athy, the little village of

Vicarstown makes an inviting place to stop with a choice of hostelries — one on either side of the canal.

Barrow Navigation — Clogrennan Lock

BARROW NAVIGATION

Athy to Levitstown

The navigation enters the River Barrow at Athy and is no longer a stillwater canal. In order to by-pass places in the river where there are shallows, canal sections, or 'cuts', were made with weirs to control the water and locks to bring the navigation down to the next level. The open weirs at the head of these cuts can be quite frightening when there is a strong flow in the river and they need to be given a wide berth. The navigation channel, or 'boat stream', as it is called, follows one or other bank of the river — the towpath is a useful indicator of your being on the correct side of it. The towpath from Athy to St Mullin's is an attractive long-distance walkway and maps are available from Cospóir.

Because of its position at an important crossing place on the River Barrow, Athy dates back to medieval times. A very handsome narrow bridge spans the river where the navigation commences and once served as a bridge for the towing horses. The second cut, past Levitstown Mill, is over 3 km (2 miles) long. Just above the mill there is a lovely old bridge which lifts horizontally, operated by a windlass. After passing under Maganey Bridge, the first of the fine old Barrow bridges to be encountered, the chimney of the sugar factory heralds the approach to Carlow.

Carlow to Milford

Carlow is the county town and, like Athy, all services can be found here. A Norman castle overlooks the river which has a fascinating history

Rathvindon Lock and the River Barrow

and the navigation swings across to the other side of the river and into the lock cut. The river banks are well wooded on the stretch to Milford, which is a pretty place with several mills, one of them approached across another picturesque lifting bridge. The river below Milford Lock is fast flowing particularly in the vicinity of islands.

Leighlinbridge to Muine Bheag

At Leighlinbridge the navigation passes under the oldest bridge on the river, which is said to date back to 1320 and is overlooked by the 16th-century Black Castle. Unable to cope with today's road traffic, a new bridge and by-pass road had to be made just upstream and so this lovely old bridge is under much less strain.

This whole area around the river is rich in sites of historical interest: there is Old Leighlin some distance from the river and below the bridge on the west bank is Ballyknockan or

Leighlinbridge

187

*Muine Bheag
lifting bridge*

Clashganna

Burgage motte built by Hugh de Lacy while Chief Governor of Ireland between 1177 and 1181.

Muine Bheag [Bagenalstown] owes its original name to Walter Bagenal, who settled here in the 18th-century. He had a grand plan to erect a town of considerable architectural splendour — an Irish Versailles — but the re-routing of the coach road through Leighlinbridge upset his plans and, although very few of the magnificent buildings

were ever built, it is a well laid-out town. Another picturesque lifting bridge, in the shadow of a large mill, gives access to the island dividing the river from the canal.

Goresbridge to Graiguenamanagh
Goresbridge has a fine stone bridge built in the mid-18th century with the village on the west bank, and the next bridge is a fine structure which

Lower Barrow

carries the road, high above the river, to nearby Borris. This is a very attractive wooded stretch of river and from here south the scenery is increasingly spectacular as the river cuts out an ever-deepening gorge. At Clashganna Lock plans are taking shape in the old mill buildings to establish a leisure and arts centre aimed largely for people with disabilities.

Lying close under Brandon Hill,

Graiguenamanagh is a picturesque town with extensive quay walls, an indication of busier times gone by. Duiske Abbey church has recently been restored and is now used again for public worship. This abbey founded in 1207 was the largest Cistercian Abbey in the country.

Downstream of the 18th-century bridge is Upper Tinnehinch lock and beside it there is a Butler castle built to defend the ford here in the past.

The Royal Canal at Kilcock

Tinnehinch to St Mullin's

The river bank on the east side is densely wooded from Upper Tinnehinch to St Mullin's Lock where the navigation passes out into tidal waters. It is a spectacularly beautiful stretch of river. The shallows at St Mullin's known as 'The Scar', can only be passed near high water and this gives time to visit the village up the hill which has many features of historical interest and associations dating back to early Celtic times (see National Monuments, p. 34). The river here is breath-takingly beautiful with steep sides, densely wooded right down to the water.

The jurisdiction of the Office of Public Works ends here and a knowledge of tidal waters and charts are needed by all who venture downstream.

THE ROYAL CANAL

The Royal Canal Aqueduct over River Boyne

The Royal Canal extends for 145 km (90 miles)

from Dublin to the upper River Shannon at Tarmonbarry and it has forty-six locks. A glance at the inland waterway map of Ireland, showing the two canals crossing the country to the Shannon from Dublin, might cause people to inquire why there are two canals. The short answer is that there never should have been two, because there was scarcely enough trade for one, but this canal was constructed in a deliberate attempt by a disgruntled former director to undermine the Grand Canal Company.

It was a much more difficult canal to construct and in many ways offers more attractive scenery than the Grand Canal. The efforts to build it not only bankrupted its originator, but also many small shareholders. Eventually when the canal had reached a point some distance west of Mullingar and funds were once again exhausted, the canal was taken over by a government authority which completed it to the Shannon. It had taken twenty-eight years to complete and the cost per mile was about £15,000 — more than double the cost of the Grand Canal.

It was never a very successful venture and, in 1845, the company sold out to the Midland and Great Western Railway Company, which used the land along the canal banks for their railway to the west. This step hastened the demise of an undertaking which had seemed doomed to failure from the start.

Closure and Restoration

Although the Royal Canal was only finally closed to navigation in 1961, boats had long since ceased to pass through it by this time. A campaign was launched in 1974 to 'Save the Royal' and the Royal Canal Amenity Group was formed, which initially confined its activities to carrying out some work clearing towpaths near Dublin. At the same time it formed itself into a pressure group, trying to prevent the lowering of any further bridges, or any other action which would make ultimate restoration more difficult.

By being seen carrying out voluntary work on

The Royal Canal Aqueduct over River Inny

the canal, by enlisting support from local communities along the line of the canal, and by commencing a lockgate construction scheme, this group managed to achieve a remarkable holding operation for it, until the upsurge in interest in the tourist and amenity potential of all waterways, swung government, local authority and public interest in their favour.

Today the restoration is in full progress, encouraged and assisted by the new administrators — the Office of Public Works. There are a number of social employment schemes in operation and lockgates are being manufactured in a FÁS, or youth training, scheme. The restoration is very much local community orientated with each place along the canal playing a role. At the moment work is concentrated on restoring the canal from the River Liffey in Dublin to Mullingar. Most of this work has been completed, almost all the levels are in-water, having been dredged, and most of the

*Ballynacargy Harbour
before restoration*

locks have been restored. When all this work has been achieved, attention will be turned to the western end of the canal. A number of low bridges on this part present some difficulties, but already a number of local communities have restored their stretches of waterway between Mullingar and the Shannon and the local authorities are beginning to take an active interest in projects.

The towpath has been cleared all the way from Dublin to Mullingar and it provides a fascinating walkway of widely differing landscapes. Sections of towpath run through woodland and other sections along open embankment. The most common landscape, however, consists of hedgerows of hawthorn, bramble and dog-rose which on closer examination, reveal a multitude of other plants. These hedge-

rows provide food and shelter for a wide variety of birds, insects, butterflies and small mammals.

The reed fringes along the canal banks also contain a wide variety of plants, providing shelter for fish and playing an important role in the ecology of the canal, supporting insects which in turn provide food for both birds and fish. The most noticeable of these water-based insects are the dragonflies and damselflies which abound in spring and early summer.

Dublin to Maynooth
The Royal Canal, like the Grand, has a large number of locks rising steeply out of the city flanked and intertwined by railways. But it quickly reaches more peaceful surroundings and it makes

*Ballynacargy Harbour
after restoration*

an interesting walk along the towpath all the way to Blanchardstown. This was the stretch of canal to which the Royal Canal Amenity Group first turned their attention when efforts to restore the canal commenced.

Leaving Blanchardstown, the canal enters a deep cutting, known as 'The Deep Sinking'. It is very narrow and, in places, the towpath is carried high above the canal. It was the scene of one of the worst accidents to a passenger boat on any Irish waterway in 1845, when a boat struck a rock near the bank, heeled over and sank with the loss of sixteen lives.

It was a difficult stretch of canal to construct and, emerging from the cutting, the canal is then carried across the River Ryewater by a massive

embankment near Leixlip. When excavating for the canal, some of the workmen discovered springs here and it became a fashionable watering place.

Maynooth to Kilcock

It is suggested that the route of the canal, bringing it close to the Grand Canal and across the Ryewater, was selected to please the Duke of Leinster, who wanted the canal to pass through his town of Maynooth. There is a fine harbour here which has now been dredged out and the canal passes along the walls of St Patrick's College, which was formerly a seminary, but now admits all students to its arts and science faculties and has university status. Its buildings and the Norman castle ruins at the entrance are of interest and well worth a visit (see National Monuments above, p. 151).

For many years motorists passing along the N4 roadway to the west saw an empty and neglected waterway at Kilcock but now it is rewatered and the harbour has been completely restored, providing a fine amenity and focus of local activities.

There are two locks in the next 4 km (2.5 miles) the sixteenth and seventeenth, both of them double, bringing the navigation up to the Long Level — 32 km (20 miles) without any locks. Fishing is good along this level with big stocks of rudd and bream.

Enfield to Mullingar
Enfield is about one-third of the way along the Long Level. The local community at Enfield have also devoted a great deal of effort to improving the canal in their vicinity. The harbour has been

*The terminus of
The Royal Canal
at Richmond Harbour*

restored with a new slip constructed here and a linear park has been made along the bank connecting the harbour area with the main road. West of Enfield the canal crosses the River Blackwater and the River Boyne. The Boyne Aqueduct is an impressive three-arched structure — one of the finest in Ireland. It is little wonder that the company encountered such financial difficulties.

The Long Level ends at Thomastown where, once again, the harbour has been restored and a new slip constructed. The canal now rises through eight locks in the space of 3.2 km (2 miles) to reach the summit level, which is some 24 km (15 miles) long, bringing the canal in a great loop around the town of Mullingar.

Western Canal
Mullingar is roughly two-thirds of the way from Dublin to the River Shannon at Clondra. There is no water in some of the stretches west of Mullingar but there are many interesting features on this part of the canal, which can be viewed from the road: a number of fine harbours at some of the villages, such as Ballynacargy, Abbeyshrule and Keenagh; the Whitworth Aqueduct over the River Inny; and a stretch of contour canal around a hill near Ballymahon, where the land rises steeply on one side and drops sharply on the other, with the waters of Lough Ree clearly visible away off to the west.

Richmond Harbour is the terminus of the Royal Canal where it joins the River Shannon. The harbour was re-watered in 1972 and boats can now lock up into it from the river. It is a very attractive place with its early 19th-century buildings which have been well-maintained.

Other useful publications:

SHELL GUIDE TO THE SHANNON
edited by Ruth Delany.

GUIDE TO THE GRAND CANAL OF IRELAND
Inland Waterways Association of Ireland.

GUIDE TO THE ROYAL CANAL OF IRELAND
Inland Waterways Association of Ireland.

Information on boat permits and current mooring and lock charges may be obtained from the Office of Public Works, 51 St. Stephen's Green, Dublin 2 — Telephone No. (01) 613111 Extension 2594.

O.P.W. Heritage Publications

The following publications are available from the
Government Publications Sales Office,
Molesworth Street, Dublin 2.

WETLANDS DISCOVERED
FARMING AND WILDLIFE
LAND MAMMALS IN IRELAND
EUROPEAN INVERTEBRATE ANIMALS
RED DATA ON VASCULAR PLANTS
PEATLANDS — AN INTRODUCTION TO BOGS
AND FENS
WILDLIFE AND THE LAW — A GUIDE TO THE
WILDLIFE ACT
IRISH FIELD MONUMENTS

Further information on National Monuments, Parks and
Gardens, Wildlife, and Inland Waterways can be obtained from
The Office of Public Works, 51 St. Stephen's Green, Dublin 2,
Ireland.

Index

(Illustrations in bold digits)